"An incredible book filled with amazing information about Italy and its splendid films! I recommend everyone who's planning a trip to Italy or simply wants a great read to grab a copy of this book. It's that good!"

*—Maria Scaretti, director of Sicilian Consortium*
*Economic Development*

"*Where Did They Film That? Italy* is an incredibly entertaining book on movie tourism, featuring movie locations with travel details on magnificent destinations in Italy. Get ready for a romantic journey to the world of films such as *Star Wars* and *Under the Tuscan Sun*. Romina Arena's book is one-of-a-kind—an absolute must if you have a love of movies and a love of travel. "

*—Svetlana Kim, spokesperson for the*
*2011 Macy's Asian Pacific Heritage Month*
*and author of* White Pearl and I:
A Memoir of a Political Refugee

"As a producer of TV specials and someone who enjoys travel, locations and sites are important to me. With Romina's book, you now have the opportunity to discover your favorite movie locations in Italy and experience the true Italian lifestyle!"

*—Stephen Disson, Disson Sports & Entertainment*

"What a wonderful journey from a woman with a personality as big as Texas taking us on a trip with the expert knowledge and expertise to guide us on an intimate excursion through a remarkable country that will make you want to revisit again and again!"

*—Stan Allen, director, Parks and Recreation,*
*City of Henderson and major concert producer*

# Where did they *film* that?

# ITALY

## FAMOUS FILM SCENES
## AND THEIR ITALIAN MOVIE LOCATIONS

## ROMINA ARENA

Fresno, California

**Where Did They Film That? ITALY**
Famous Film Scenes and Their Italian Movie Locations

Published by Quill Driver Books,
an imprint of Linden Publishing
2006 South Mary, Fresno, California 93721
559-233-6633 / 800-345-4447
QuillDriverBooks.com

Quill Driver Books and Colophon are trademarks
of Linden Publishing, Inc.

ISBN 978-1-61035-182-9

Printed in the United States
First Printing

The author and publisher have endeavored to provide in this book the most up-to-date information available. However, as details are subject to change, the author and publisher cannot accept responsibility for any consequences or injuries arising from the use of this book.

Library of Congress Cataloging-in-Publication Data on file

# Contents

# Dedication

This book is dedicated to the most wonderful and inspiring woman I have ever met, my "bestest of the friendests," Renae Wright. You are so very important to me, Renae—I want you to remember that forever. This book is for you! My heart is filled with love and gratitude, and I thank you from the depths of my heart for being in my life.

I also dedicate this book to my mama, Rita, who taught me from a young age to embrace different cultures and countries and who took me all over the world. Grazie mamma! Ti amo infinitamente!

And this book is also dedicated to Jay Hall, my manager and companion through many crazy adventures around the world. Jay, you make my journeys truly unforgettable. Thank you for helping me and supporting me with this one!

*A gorgeous view of Piazza San Marco in, Venice, Italy. PHOTO BY JAY HALL*

# Acknowledgments

First and foremost I would love to thank God for allowing me each day to live this splendid journey and adventure called life. I cannot ever, not even for a second, take for granted a brand new day. Thank you, God, for giving me eyes to see the colors of nature, ears to listen to the sounds of the ocean, legs to walk through breathtaking lands, and a voice so that I can inspire others to go out there and enjoy life fully!

**carpe diem....**

I would like to thank the many organizations and individuals who supported me throughout the making of this book. Your love and belief mean everything to me.

My thanks go out to my exciting new record company, Lakeshore Records. In particular, my thanks go to Brian McNellis, head of the label and music supervisor extraordinaire, who had a vision to turn this book into music, allowing me to record the most beautiful theme songs from films shot in Italy. For all of you fans of Italy and of music—do not forget to pick a copy of *Where Did They Film That? Italy—the Music Journey*!

From the bottom of my heart, I thank the great Oscar-winning film composer Maestro Ennio Morricone for allowing me to work with him in writing lyrics and recording to his music. My deep thanks also to the brilliant film composer, Maestro Nicola Piovani, winner of an Academy Award for *Life Is Beautiful*, who granted me permission to record "Beautiful That Way"—and to his brother, Nino Piovani.

Deep thanks also to the mesmerizing Italian director and Golden Globe winner Gian Paolo Cugno, who allowed me to dig into his research box to draw a picture of Sicily that I'd almost forgotten. Thank you for bringing our Sicily to the world in such a picturesque and superb way. Your movies are pure poetry in motion!

To the inspirational Vincenzo Arcobelli, the Sicilian Confederation of North America, and the Italian American community, thank you for having faith in all the things that I do. Vincenzo, you are a true guardian angel in my life. This book is a symbol of devotion and love for our country, Italy, and I look forward to building a platform with you so that others can embrace our culture through schools, classes, and more Italian-related events in the United States.

Of course, my deep thanks and dedication go to the leading force in my life, the great Renae Marie Wright, for her endless love and support, believing in me when no one else did. You have my heart forever! "That's what Friends are for"

A special thanks goes to my amazing manager, Jay Hall, for always being my safe port and a solid companion in my life and career adventures. Any artist would be lucky to have you, but I got luckier!

I thank my dedicated and brilliant vice-president of creative productions at Arena Sonic Brand Company, Regina Randolph. Your dedication to me and my company for the last fifteen years has made such a difference in my personal and business life. Regina, it is because of you that I go on, because as you taught me, "I walk by faith, not by sight!" Thank you for your amazing editing skills and marvelous contributions.

I also want to thank two precious women who have also been in my life for years and now are supporting the mission statement of Romina Arena Worldwide and Arena Sonic Brand while helping me to accomplish the impossible. They are my executive assistant and director of operations, Hazel Suarez, for her dedication to my career and company (you are brilliant and my shining star—never forget that), and Diana Hart, for her constant belief in me.

To my dear friend and trusted family attorney, Tim Devik, thanks for advising me always to do the right thing. Your integrity is so thick that I can cut it with a knife! Thanks to my incredibly passionate and knowledgeable entertainment lawyer, Brad Rubens; I am so glad you are back in my life, building a protective wall in this (I hate to say it) cutthroat business.

Special thanks to all the following (you know why): Al Pacino, Giuseppe Tornatore, Franco Turdo, Titti and Ninni Luparello, Veronica Gozzi, and Linda Sposati. Thanks to Francis Ford Coppola, the Italian Institute of culture, the Italian consulates of Los Angeles and Washington, DC, Los Angeles Mayor Eric Garcetti, the National Italian American Foundation, the Sons of Italy, Unico, and Ed Asner.

Thanks to my father for his indirect way of showing me a love for photography. I can see clearly now! It's almost like a funny game of words, but through the "negatives" of your photography, I have found the "positive" forces to do this guide. You will be forever missed.

I'm grateful to all the media involved in this project—magazines, blogs, vlogs, newspapers, radio, and social media—for allowing me to reach so many people with this book. In particular, I want to thank *Tastes of Italia*, *Generoso d'Agnese*, *The Times of Sicily* and Professor D'Alessandro, Alan McBride and the Florida Broadcasting Company, **PRIMO** magazine, and *People* magazine.

Thanks, of course, to all the hotels, cruise lines, restaurants, sponsors, and licensing partners that supported this fantastic journey of rediscovery in Italy. You have been instrumental in enabling me to find the very best in all that you represent. I am honored to call you partners. In particular, I'd like to thank Joerg Felten of the car rental company Avis for providing my team with the most excellent car service anywhere in Italy. I especially thank Joerg for his endless support and belief in this project. I highly recommend Avis to my readers; their professionalism and care have made all the difference during my travels. It's a wonderful thing to travel abroad and be stress free!

I thank my book publishers, Kent Sorsky and Richard Sorsky, their brilliant marketing associate, Jaguar, as well as Heather and the rest of the Linden Publishing/Quill Driver Books family for believing in this project and supporting me every step of the way. Thank you for giving me the chance to bring my ideas to life! Because of you, now I can take others along with me to the places I find so incredible.

Most importantly, my thanks go to my growing fan base, for supporting me and believing in me for years as an international recording artist, performer, and motivational speaker. Hopefully you will support me as an author, too. I hope my words will inspire you to travel the globe, discovering the beautiful things life can bring. Don't wait! The future is promised to no one—all that counts is today, so go out there in the world and explore.

*Romina Arena in concert in Las Vegas.* PHOTO BY DAVID MAGOUN (FULL SPECTRUM ARTS & SERVICES)

# Welcome to My Country, Italy

*"Twenty years from now you will be more disappointed by the things that you didn't do than by the ones you did do. So throw off the bowlines. Sail away from the safe harbor. Catch the trade winds in your sails. Explore. Dream. Discover."* —MARK TWAIN

## BUONGIORNO AMICI!

It is truly thrilling to introduce you to the country where I was born. Italy is a wonderful combination of colorful people, traditions, customs, saints—a beautiful concoction of old and new, a country that looks to the future but remains anchored to the ancient rules of hospitality, harmony, and traditional values. Italy embraces you with love and passion.

Everything is pure passion in Italy! We are born this way.

*Italy is renowned for its gorgeous landscapes, historic cities, and culture of hospitality and enjoyment of life.*

*Piazza Venezia, in Rome. Italy is a nation with a proud history, culture, and way of life.*

Italians are naturally bubbly people, with much to give and to say.

It's not by chance that directors and producers from all over the world have chosen Italy as the backdrop for their film creations. There's something profound about Italy; it's an intricate combination of the mystical and the magical, grabbing your heart and never letting go. Italy is pure poetry and music—you can see it, hear it, and feel it everywhere. From street markets to beaches to ancient ruins, everything whispers to you, sings to you, fills you with pleasure. That's why many people have come to Italy and never left. Some just cannot live without it.

And to me, Italy is like a mother who waits for her child to come home, always with wide-open arms. You can sense the warmth, the nurturing essence of a mother and the enchanting look that never grows old. Have you ever had the feeling of walking on clouds to someplace out of this world? Each time I return to Italy, a great whirl of emotions and pleasure comes over me, giving me a new sense of discovery. It's magical to arrive in the old country and completely surrender yourself to the enchantment of the Mediterranean, to lose the measure of time and space at the ancient monuments.

You may think that talking about Italy is an easy thing for me to do, given my background. In reality, after living in the United States for more than eighteen

*Siena Cathedral, in Siena. Italian cities offer amazing experiences of history and beauty.*

years, I realized that I felt like a perfect tourist when I returned home to work on this book. All the things I discovered, after traveling to Italy for research about the place where I was born, were new and exciting to me. What an amazing feeling, to sway to the sound of that music, to soak in the sacred history, and to explore things I hadn't imagined even existed in Italy.

Probably because I lived in Italy until I was seventeen years old before moving away to America, when I returned home to my mother I was as excited as a child about to open her holiday gifts. I decided to let go of some of the things I thought I knew about Italy and start from scratch. I even asked questions in English sometimes, because I wanted to experience both sides of the coin—as the Italian who knows her country and as a foreigner ready to explore a new land. I wanted to be like a painter with a white canvas and a thousand colors at my disposal, so that I could paint my own vision of this country. I decided to approach it with the eyes of a *bambina*—a little girl—with wonder and enthusiasm. You should do the same!

## A DIFFERENT—AND PERSONAL—VIEW OF ITALY

From one of the most beautiful beaches in the entire world at Sabaudia—the beach of the Greek gods—to the spicy, sweet scents of Sicily and the lush elegance of Tuscany, Italy has something to offer everyone. The true spirit of Italy comes alive in the exploration of small villages, ancient areas that the Italians call "places where Jesus lost his shoes"—places so forgotten or unfamiliar that not even Jesus could find them!

Jokes aside, such destinations are often even more fantastic than the better-known sites on typical itineraries. And these are exactly the places I will show you!

A great many books have been written about Italy, but I want to bring you something different. As you can see, this isn't a thick and overwhelming tourist's guide; there are already many excellent guidebooks, and you should definitely buy one if you're planning to visit Italy. My book is a romantic invitation to visit the locations of favorite movies (I'm a huge movie fan!) and, most importantly, to embrace the lifestyle of a people who really know how to live life. Italians have cracked the code for finding the time to love, to eat, and to sleep, the three simple ingredients for pure happiness. Come away with me on a journey to the land of love, where music, beauty, and inspiration are filling people's lives every day!

And what about those beautiful movies that have touched us so deeply? How many of us have dreamed of experiencing those unique moments played to perfection by our favorite actors—the innocent Audrey Hepburn in *Roman Holiday*, the adventurous Julia Roberts in *Eat Pray Love*, sweet Kristen Stewart and Robert Pattinson in *The Twilight Saga: New Moon*?

I've been in love with the world of movies ever since I was a little girl. I later poured my cinematic adoration into the music, so I began to write songs to become a film composer. I would watch the same movies over and over again to capture every detail of the story and the soundtrack, focusing first on the music and then on the locations. That ignited in me a love for creating scenarios in my own head. I was always asking myself what had helped the director to make

the right choices for a specific movie or scene. So I started to research great movies and their locations.

My love for the silver screen and my love of travel got me to thinking that I should pull these two things together so that you could visit your favorite movie settings and at the same time take part in the Italian philosophy of life.

Food has always been a fundamental part of Italy and of the many movies made there. Through inviting camera shots, directors and screenwriters try to duplicate the sense of tasting that delicious spaghetti or incredible pizza. And while Julia Roberts was gaining weight in *Eat Pray Love*, all of us watching her were in food heaven as well, imagining how incredible that food might taste. Well, of course, I *already* know, but I want you to experience it, too! That's why I'm offering a few delicious recipes in this book, so that you can re-create

the taste of Italy when you go back home.

And because I truly believe that there is no life without music, I'm suggesting favorite film tracks for you to listen to, so that mentally you can be in Italy anytime. (You can

*Authentic Italian cuisine is renowed throughout the world— and is simply delicious!*

also listen to the companion album to this book, *Where Did They Film That? Italy—the Music Journey*, available on my website, RominaArena.com.)

I know that many of us love to know about exceptional places, so in this volume I tell you about the best of the best. I've included some top luxury hotels (not hundreds, just a handful representing the very best), selected for their service, elegance, uniqueness, and food. I've suggested some divine restaurants, too, and an amazing cruise. This book is a personally guided tour by an authentic Italian into the core of the land, that will help you experience the country's pleasures while you step into scenes from your favorite movies.

*One of the world's great tourist destinations, Italy is perfect for every–thing from viewing the world's greatest art to lounging on the beach.*

## THE ROAD TO DISCOVERY

My mother and dad had a strong love of photography, and as a young couple, before I came along, they traveled the world discovering and photographing the most remarkable things. I was only four years old when my dad left us. At that young age I became a ballerina, a singer, and a constant traveler—one of the gifts from my mother that I most appreciate and thank her for. Being exposed to the world transformed me into a powerful cosmopolitan, hungry for knowledge, a connoisseur of the pleasures life has to offer around the world and always thirsting to learn about different cultures and languages. Today, thanks to my mother and our travels together, I speak ten languages.

At only ten years of age, I had already traveled much of the world. Now in my thirties, I can say with joy and pride that I have traveled through Europe, Australia, New Zealand, Mexico, the United States, Canada, Japan, and Thailand. Of course, there are many incredible places that I still want to see, unknown cultures and ways of life that I want to experience.

Take your children on long expeditions, so they will grow up with an invincible spirit of exploration and become open to new horizons. It is so gratifying and enjoyable to share experiences of this kind with family, growing together and raising the bar. Just do it!

I believe that traveling the world changes a person. Finding yourself in a foreign country, surrounded by people you don't necessarily understand, isn't as scary as we sometimes think it will be. It's just a step into a world of possibilities.

Many people wait until late in life to explore the world. Don't wait to move outside your comfort zone! I know that people work very hard to save money for travel, but there are many options these days. Travel companies offer endless deals to anywhere you want to go. Money comes and money goes; don't wait too long to hop onto a plane. Grab your children, spouse, lover, mom, or dad, and share the power of discovery. It's so much fun! It has a delicious taste, it makes you feel alive. When you return home, your view of things—even in your regular daily routine—will be completely different. You will feel mentally richer.

Traveling the world is an enriching experience. Find your own road to discovery. Now!

Use this guide as a source of inspiration. I hope that it will entice you to visit Italy many times, exploring the places where great scenes from movies were filmed—or even to fall in love and get married! I hope that in these pages you will find many interesting things to do, and that you'll uncover details you didn't know about Italian culture. And I hope that you'll return home with a desire to learn more—and to use this book over and over again.

*Benvenuti* to Italy!

---

**TRAVEL TIP**

Don't try to see or do everything in one trip! (Which is impossible anyway.) That's why this book suggests a lot of great things to see in my country, but not *everything*. Sometimes less is best. It's preferable to focus on only a couple of regions or cities. Just one of them will be enough to keep you busy for at least a couple of weeks. Trust me—Italy is filled with surprises.

# 2

# The Italian Experience

*"You will, if you're wise and know the art of travel, let yourself go on the stream of the unknown and accept whatever comes in the spirit in which the gods may offer it."* —FREYA STARK

Let me just say that I adore Italy—not because I'm Italian, but because the people are nice, the food is delicious, and there's always something new to discover. The fashion, the cars, the people, the food: things Italian have made quite a difference in the culture of the world. And there is no other place where you can find such abundance of culture and beauty.

I know I am a bit biased, but what can I do? This is my beloved land, and I know that when you visit my home country you will learn to love it as yours. To help you to get the most out of your Italian experience, in this chapter I want to offer a few tips and insights into my country. Travel here with an open mind and an open heart.

*Salute!* Enjoy!

## A COUNTRY OF DRAMA

Italy is gorgeous, but it's also noisy, full of temperamental people who yell at each other like bloody murder. Don't worry, that's just the way they talk—with passion and zest. They're not actually fighting. No hard feelings for them, so there's no reason for you to be frightened or concerned. They're loud, but what you want to avoid is being loud *with* them. At that point, everything will turn into something like an Italian comedy or drama, as they might think you have a problem with them!

Because Italy is a country of drama, sometimes you'll encounter strikes, so the trains might not be running. Don't panic! Go to the train station, and you'll find additional trains or other means of transportation to take you to your destination. Everything will work out.

Always remember that Italy is all about passion, so be ready to jump into any new occasion that presents itself. It's so important to let your guard down and embrace new possibilities.

## THE QUESTION OF LANGUAGE

The younger generations in Italy speak pretty good English, but Italians over the age of

**TRAVEL TIP** Get started early in the morning when you're in Italy if you can, because it's great to see the dawn and enjoy the day. Try to have what I call a "wandering day," where you don't really follow any traditional itinerary. Actually, the more you wander without measuring time, place, and space, the more exciting it's going to be. Discovering little villages, historical sites, or food parlors hidden away in vineyards is just so wonderful. Don't be afraid to try new things. You'll rejuvenate yourself and approach life in a whole new way.

*Starting at sunrise will give you a full day to enjoy Italy.*

fifty barely chew the language. They do want to communicate and understand what you are saying, though, so be sure to learn a few phrases in Italian. Here are a few to get you started:

- *Buongiorno* (Good morning)
- *Perfavore* (Please)
- *Buona notte* (Good night)
- *Come stai?* (How are you?)
- *Parla inglese?* (Do you speak English?)

When you talk to Italians, please don't start a conversation by speaking in English—you'll be looked at as if you're a Martian. It's actually a great idea to carry a dictionary or an electronic translation device so that you can always find that one word you're looking for, when you need it.

## A FEW POINTS OF ETIQUETTE

Here are a few pointers to help you to be in step with the Italian way of doing things during your visit:

- Always be polite when you walk into a store. Say *buongiorno* or *buona sera* ("good morning" or "good evening").
- Don't expect Italians on the street to chat with you out of the blue or to say hello the way we do in America. They are like bears living in their own little caves; they may feel shy, so say *buongiorno* first and everything will work out well.

- If you are at a grocery store, wait your turn to order or pay for food. Don't be offended or overwhelmed if no one is providing for you yet. The owners aren't ignoring you, they are just paying attention to the customers before you, one person at the time. Your turn will come, and then you will notice the same thing: they will dedicate their time to you and ask the next customer to be patient.
- Tipping a waiter in a restaurant is not something that Italians usually do or expect. This doesn't mean we're not appreciative of the hard work that waiters do, but usually their tips are included in the final bill. You can always add something extra if you feel that your server has done an especially good job, but do so in style and on the side, as those working alongside your waiter might be resentful that they didn't receive a tip. So be discreet.
- When you go out to eat, please dress well and be presentable. Don't be sloppy. Waiters won't respect you

*Expect a hearty welcome at Italian restaurants, especially if you're polite.*

if you don't present yourself as a decent human being. Dress nicely when you visit churches or museums; don't wear shorts and sandals, as if you're going to the beach. Have you noticed that Italians are always well dressed and elegant? Learn from this example, at least when you're not headed to the beach, and you'll be allowed to go everywhere.

- Make sure you don't put your feet up on a chair or on the table in public, and don't make any strange, loud noises (such as blowing your nose too loudly). Be respect-

### Did You Know?

- Italians will never put chicken, pineapple, or other extras on their pizza, even if you ask for them. It's almost an insult, so stick with what's on the menu when you go to the local pizzeria.

- Italians are required to give part of their wages to the Church. That share gets paid even before people receive their pay.

- Italians consider both the color purple and the number 17 to be bad luck.

ful of others and they will respect you. Italians are very judgmental and "old school." They might *look* ahead of the times, but their culture, mentality, and history make them hold close to old ways of dealing with situations.

- When in conversation with Italians, steer away from talking about politics (especially American policy) or war. You'll start your own war if you talk about these hot topics, as the Italians' passion may become almost unbearable!

One subject to avoid is the Mafia. Although Mafia often is identified with Italy (thanks to some of the movies out there, I hate to say), we all know that criminality is just about everywhere. Italians truly suffer from these remarks, and I personally feel the weight of all of this, because I'm Sicilian. Despite the curiosity Americans have about Mafia stories, the best thing to do while you're in Italy is to not engage in this topic of conversation. You won't be appreciated if you do and you'll end up offending people, so pay attention…or else! (Unless, of course, they make you an offer you can't refuse.)

A very silly person once asked me, because I was from the land of the Mafia, if I handled guns or knives. "Both!" I answered, out of frustration. Of course we don't go around killing people, or taking advantage of them or hurting them. I believe that bad people and good people are everywhere. But Italians are hard workers, honest and loving people, dedicated to their work, their homes, their values, and most importantly their families.

## ITALY AT NIGHT

Pace yourself so that you can stay up at night when you're in Italy. Nighttime is the bewitching time for an Italian, and Italy is famous for its nightlife. Italian men and women don't worry if they miss work the day after, or if they get to work late; no, they don't worry! They love to walk around in their cities at night, especially in the areas where the promenade is located. Italians just love to spend time out at night.

*Italian monuments are even more dramatic by night. The Altar of the Fatherland, also known as the National Monument to Victor Emmanuel II, first king of united Italy.*

## Land of Romance—and Impossible Love

*"Obstacles cannot crush me. Every obstacle yields to stern resolve. He who is fixed to a star does not change his mind."* — LEONARDO DA VINCI

Since we'll be focusing on movies as we travel through Italy, it's natural to consider some of the most iconic figures when it comes to matters of the heart.

We're all familiar with the tragedy of the impossible love in *Romeo and Juliet*, Shakespeare's play set in Verona (see Chapter 5). But what about the adorable little angel with the arrow that always hits us right in the heart of our senses? Cupid, from the old Latin *Cupido* (and still called this in Italian), is the god of love—*il dio dell'amore*. There's an old story that tells how Cupid prompted Dido to fall in love with Aeneas, with terrible consequences. But in Roman tradition and legend, Cupid was the son of Venus, goddess of love, and Mars, god of war. Cupid is still considered a powerful character who represents eternal love, and you'll find little cupids everywhere in Italian paintings and sculptures.

Now let's talk about another tragic Shakespearean love story that takes place partly in Italy, *Antony and Cleopatra*. (Shakespeare must have loved Italy!) Definitely a real person, Cleopatra was born in 69 BC, the last of the Ptolemies—the Macedonian-descended pharaohs who'd ruled Egypt since 304 BC. Popular for her ambition and determination, Cleopatra won the heart of the Roman emperor Julius Caesar and had a son with him, Caesarion. After Caesar's death, Cleopatra joined forces with his colleague Marc Antony to keep control of her kingdom; they became lovers and political allies against Caesar's nephew Octavian, who'd been named heir to the emperor in place of Caesarion. When Octavian's forces defeated those of Antony and Cleopatra in 31 BC, the lovers committed suicide. Legend has it that Cleopatra died by snakebite, though there's actually no proof of that.

Of course, this extraordinary story had to find its way onto the screen. The history is just unbelievable! The filming of the movie *Cleopatra* began in England, but after star Elizabeth Taylor (Cleopatra, of course) became dangerously ill, production was moved to Cinecitta Studios in Rome to escape the harsh English weather. The extravagant movie sets had to be built all over again when the filming moved to Italy.

You'll want to check out the exquisite musical score created by composer Alex North for the movie.

## CLEOPATRA

RELEASE: 1963     DIRECTOR: Joseph L. Mankiewicz
CAST: Elizabeth Taylor, Richard Burton, Rex Harrison, Roddy McDowall, Martin Landau

### Movie Trivia

- Female extras playing Cleopatra's servants and slave girls went on strike to demand protection from bottom-pinching Italian male extras. The studio eventually hired security guards for the women.
- Actor Martin Landau, who had the role of Rufio, learned Italian during the filming of the movie.
- At Cinecitta Studios, the filming of Cleopatra's triumphant entry into Rome required thousands of extras and the transporting of a huge barge. But the director had to stop production and reshoot the scene after he noticed that one of the extras was eating gelato and sharing it with other extras, all of them dressed in Roman costume. Quite hilarious!

*Elizabeth Taylor in* Cleopatra *(1963).*

And if you want to do something very special, go swimming in the Mediterranean at night, under the moon and the stars. I grew up this way, and I wish I could do that in the Pacific Ocean at Malibu, where I live—but it's too cold. So let's stick with Italy, shall we?

## DRIVERS TAKE HEED

If you decide to drive in Italy, don't try to keep up with Italian drivers—they will always win! Italians drive like there's no tomorrow. They are used to driving extremely close to one another, and up onto the curbs. My own mother gives me a heart attack when I go to Palermo and she drives me around. I feel like I'm riding the bumper cars at the theme park, except that this is about my survival. Please don't laugh, I'm serious!

If you want to challenge yourself, then do that; just be kind on the road and drive in safe areas. One of my favorite drives is along the Amalfi coast (see Chapter 8). But what are you doing, still listening to me? Just go and try it!

## FAST FOOD? TRY SLOW FOOD!

The famous Mediterranean diet keeps Italians healthy and gives them longevity. Italians have even created the opposite of fast food. A movement called Slow Food was started in Italy in 1986, and since then it has spread to other countries as well. You might want to become part of this exciting movement—visit slowfood.com to learn more about it.

The same philosophy works for travelers. Check slowtrav.com to find out how you can immerse yourself in the *dolce*

*far niente*—the sweetness of doing nothing!

## THE HOLIDAYS IN ITALY

Traveling in Italy during the winter holiday season can be an unforgettable experience. Here are some of the ways the holidays are traditionally celebrated here:

- At Christmas, the entire Italian boot is covered in lights, with big feasts in the street and fireworks everywhere. You'll see the *presepe*, the Nativity scene, all over Italy.
- Over the Christmas holidays, Italians consume both *panettone*, a sweet bread with candied fruit, and *pandoro*, a similar but softer bread covered with powder sugar. Simply delicious!
- Churches throughout the country—including the beautifully decorated Vatican—celebrate midnight Mass on Christmas Eve. And you'll be pleased to find that in the big cities (such as Rome and Milan), the Mass is spoken in multiple languages, including English.
- Most Italians use a lot of red at New Year's time, as it's supposed to bring good fortune. In fact, Italians typically wear a new pair of red underwear on New Year's Eve!
- The New Year's Eve meal traditionally includes lentils, to bring prosperity during the coming year.
- Epiphany takes over from January 2 through 8. This is one of the favorite holiday

**TRAVEL TIP**

When you are walking around museums and shopping centers, at some point you'll most likely need use to the bathroom. If none of the places you're visiting has a restroom available, my suggestion is to walk into a bar and pay for an espresso or a little something to eat so that you have an excuse to use their restroom. If you don't do that, your request will be declined, and you'll be in worse trouble than ever. You want to say something like this: *un espresso per favore*? (an espresso, please?); then add *Il bagno per favore*? (the restroom, please?), and you'll have access to that magic little place of relief.

Each time you walk into an Italian bathroom, next to the toilet you'll find a matching ceramic fixture. That's the *bidè*, and you're supposed to use it after you use the toilet to—how shall I say?— freshen your private parts. You're not obligated to use it (not everyone does), but it's there for your convenience!

celebrations for Italian children, right after Christmas itself. They receive presents from a flying witch called *La Befana* rather than from Santa Claus. Italians don't even know who Santa is, unless you're referring to a saint or you use the name *Babbo Natale* (Father Christmas).

## Holiday High Season

You should be aware that you'll be subject to "mini high season" rates at holiday time, wherever you go in Italy. Hotels and bed and breakfasts places usually charge three times their regular rates over the holidays.

Also, most banks and government offices have restricted hours during holiday times, and some may be closed. Even public transportation may operate on a limited schedule. Plan ahead. You can buy train tickets in advance, for example, and bring extra food to your hotel room or apartment so you don't get stuck if restaurants are closed.

**TRAVEL TIP**

**Talking Turkey**
Italians don't observe Thanksgiving, so don't try to find a place that will serve you turkey or pumpkin pie; they'll look at you very strangely!

*This view of St. Peter's Basilica from the tiber river shows some the eternal characteristics of Italian culture—classic architecture, elegant urban planning, and the heritage of centuries of history as the center of the civilized world.*

# 3

# The Boot and Beyond

*"Avoiding danger is no safer in the long run than outright exposure. Life is either a daring adventure or nothing."* —HELEN KELLER

I've always wondered why, when I ask American tourists where they went when they visited Italy, I hear the same answers: Rome, Venice, Florence, Naples, the Amalfi coast. I know these destinations are spectacular, but I rarely hear about Calabria, Sicily, and Sardinia, and these are truly magical spots.

Most travel guides or organized tours will take you through the Italian boot, but most likely no one will suggest that you venture off the mainland to explore the luscious islands of Sicily and Sardinia. It's almost a sin, not knowing about these gorgeous places! (You can contact the Where Did They Film That? Italy tour office in Los Angeles at (323) 798-8854 to have our team prepare a tour to any region of Italy, including the movie locations mentioned in this book.)

## SICILY—IT'S NOT A SEPARATE COUNTRY

Many Americans—and even Italian Americans, unfortunately —think that Sicily isn't part of Italy but is a country per se. This couldn't be further from the truth. Sicily has always been part of Italy. This gorgeous island is where I grew up, and I invite you to explore it in all its natural beauty. You will feel so rejuvenated here—and you

The town of Cefalu in Sicily.

may be surprised by how many movies have been shot in Sicily.

## THE ISLAND OF SARDINIA

For Italians, Sardinia—or Sardegna, as we call it—is another magnificent gift of God to earth. The modern, rich coastal resort areas of Costa Smeralda, Costa Verde, and Porto Cervo are exquisite, and you'll be completely blown away by the beauty and allure of this island.

Sardinia provided the backdrop for the 2002 Madonna movie *Swept Away*, directed by Guy Richie, as well as some of the spaghetti westerns.

The spectacular **Costa Verde** resort area—the "Green Coast"—is in southwestern Sardinia, centered at Arbus. To reach it, you can fly to Cagliari Elmas airport in the south, the airport of Alghero Fertilia in the northwest, or Olbia Costa Smeralda in the northeast. If you're arriving by sea, the ports are Cagliari, Olbia, and Porto Torres. For information about Costa Verde, visit lacostaverde. eu.

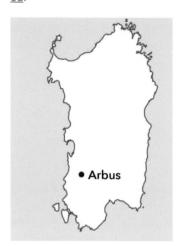

The chic and luxurious area of Porto Cervo is where a great many VIPs spend their summers. Here are some of the best places to stay:

**CERVO HOTEL**
The delightful accommodations are airy, cheerful, and bright, overlooking the harbor and the town square. The elegant hotel has a conference center and several restaurants.
*Costa Smeralda*
*Porto Cervo 07020*
**Website:** *hotelcervo costasmeralda.com*
**Phone:** *+39 0789 931111*

**HOTEL CALA DI VOLPE**
Another wonderful five-star hotel in the same area.
*Costa Smeralda*
*Porto Cervo 07020*

One way to soak up local color is to take in one of the many events that take place in Sardinia throughout the summer. Here are a few of them:

**Saint Anthony of Padua Celebration**—During this June 12–15 celebration, a statue of the saint is carried by ox-drawn cart from Arbus to Sant'Antonio di Santadi in a procession of costumed knights and the walking faithful. Various folkloric and gastronomic events take place.

**Arresojas**—Sardinia is well known for artisan knives, and

## Romina's Hotel Picks

**Website:** *caladivolpe.com*
**Phone:** *+39 0789 976111*
And if you feel like Donald Trump or want to mingle with the richest people in the area, you can join the famous Yacht Club of Costa Smeralda—a fantastic place to swim, rent a boat, and meet some very powerful people.

**YACHT CLUB COSTA SMERALDA**
*Associazione Sportiva Dilettantistica*
*Via della Marina*
*07021 Porto Cervo*
**Website:** *yccs.it*
*Phone: +39 0789 902200*

*Super-yachts of the super-wealthy in Costa Smeralda, Sardinia.*

the tourist authority of Guspini organizes this forged cutlery fair in the mining village of Montevecchio biennially in late July/early August.

**Blessed Virgin Bonaria Celebration**—On the second Sunday after August 15, fishermen carry a statue of the Madonna onto the sea from the village of Marceddì to ask for protection and a blessing of the boats.

**Fish Feast**—The August fish feast in Buggerru offers a chance to enjoy fresh local fish and the Sardinian fish soup called *cassola*, together with excellent locally produced wines such as Monica, Vermentino, and Sulcis Carignano.

**Honey Fair**—The town of Montevecchio hosts a late-summer festival where you can taste honeys and confections traditionally made in the region. Visitors can also tour mining sites.

## THE TOE OF THE BOOT

Calabria is all the way south at the tip of the Italian boot. When I was investigating what movies have been filmed here, I was surprised to learn that there haven't been many—but I still believe that you should come and explore this beautiful region! Not discovering Calabria would truly be a loss.

The following cultural and tourism office is responsible for the city of **Reggio Calabria**. There are English speakers

there who can help you learn about this beautiful region. You're going to fall in love with this place!

### Reggio Calabria Tourism Office

Via Fata Morgana 13
89125 Reggio Calabria
Website: tourismo.reggiocal.it
Phone: +39 0965 324822

## A LAND OF LAKES

Italy is a country of stunning lakes, and each one—just like each individual person—has its own unique character. The personality and beauty of **Lake Garda**, the largest, are different from the particular elegance and charm of **Lake Como** (see Chapter 5). You will be quite astonished by these beautiful places, I can assure you, even if you come from America's land of 10,000 lakes, Minnesota! Charming little steamboats and other vessels navigate the waters. If you're planning a family event, one of these lakes might be just the right setting—or the ideal spot for what the Italians call *la luna di miele*, the most perfect honeymoon!

## THE COUNTRY LIFE

If you're an outdoor-oriented person—or simply want a taste of Italy's rural life—you might want to take part in Italy's *agriturismo* business. That means staying on family-owned farms, perhaps riding horses, enjoying healthy meals featuring local products—and maybe even living a life of luxury, because these days a farmhouse may come with a masseuse, swimming pool, and private chef!

The air is great, the food wholesome, and the scenery unforgettable. This could be just what you need if you spend the rest of your year in the city. Sipping delicious wine, surrounded by green fields and old vineyards, enjoying local cheeses and listening to Italian opera—or Romina Arena!—what more could you ask for? Many of the farms that participate in the *agriturismo* program are in Tuscany, Umbria, and Macerata.

*Agriturismo is a fun and delicious way to discover the roots of Italian cuisine.*

*The historic town of Bellagio, set in picturesque Lake Como.*

### Did You Know?

- The most amazing time of rebirth for Italy was the fervent Renaissance era, beginning in the 14th century in Florence with such artistic giants as Michelangelo. (For more about Florence and Michelangelo, turn to Chapter 11.) But the Renaissance was more than breathtaking statues and artwork. Italians even created an "ideal" Renaissance city called Palmanova, in far northeastern Italy. If you were to look at it from above, you'd see a perfect artistic design spreading out in a nine-pointed star. Begun in 1593, Palmenova was designed as a self-sustaining citadel city. The only problem? No one wanted to settle there.

*An aerial view of Palmanova, a rationally planned city founded during the Renaissance.*

- There's an Italian city called Campione d'Italia that lies completely outside of Italy, entirely surrounded by Switzerland. Situated on the shore of Lake Lugano, the city is less than a mile from Italy's northern border, but because of the mountainous terrain you have to drive about 9 miles to get there from the nearest town in Italy, Lanzo d'Intelvi.

*The cliffs at Tropea in Calabria present a dramatic confrontation between the land and the sea.*

# 4

# Practical Matters

*"The world is a book and those who do not travel read only a page."* —St. Augustine

## TRAVEL DOCUMENTS

U.S. citizens need only a valid passport to enter Italy for a stay of up to 90 days. Information on how and where to obtain a passport is available from the U.S. Department of State by going to travel.state.gov/passport or by calling (877) 487-2778.

Before you travel, make two copies of your passport's data page, one to leave with someone at home and another to carry yourself, separate from your actual passport. You can also scan the page and email it to someone at home and/or yourself. This is a perfect way to protect yourself in case you lose your documents and need proof of identity. I've heard stories of people getting stuck in other countries because they lacked proof of their citizenship, so come prepared.

If you plan to be in Italy for longer than 90 days, you'll need to obtain a visa from an Italian consulate before you leave the United States. (Allow at least 30 days for this.) Consulates are also good sources of other information about Italy. All the Italian consulates in the United States are listed on the Embassy of Italy website, www.ambwashingtondc.esteri.it.

## MONEY MATTERS

The euro is the main unit of currency in Italy and 18 other European countries. The system is pretty simple. There are 100 *centesimi* (cents) to the euro. Notes come in 5, 10, 20, 50, 100, 200, and 500-euro amounts; coins have 1, 2, 5, 10, 20, and 50-centesimi and 1 and 2-euro values.

*Euro bills and coins are colorful and easy to understand—and they're legal tender in all nineteen Eurozone countries, including Italy.*

At publication time for this book, €1 was worth about $1.09 in U.S. dollars. Post offices exchange currency at excellent rates, but hardly anyone there will speak English. Writing your request on a piece of paper can help overcome the language barrier. You might want to exchange some money at your own bank before you leave home, or with an Italian bank when you get to Italy. When you exchange money in Italy, be prepared for additional fees and taxes.

Be sure to call your bank and credit card companies prior to traveling outside the United States to let them know you'll be using your debit and credit cards overseas. I had a bad experience once, finding myself unable to access my account for three days because I hadn't alerted my bank that I was going out of town.

ATMS are available everywhere, operating 24 hours a day. But be ready for a hefty extra charge each time you

*Italian trains are fast, efficient, and pass through some of the most beautiful landscapes on earth.*

draw cash from your account; check your bank's policy ahead of time. Of course, you should always be extremely careful with your cards and your PINs; there are too many scammers in this world!

Your credit cards and debit cards will usually be accepted at most retail outlets in Italy, including train stations and stores. But don't assume that a restaurant or bar will accept credit cards; most of them won't. Traveler's cheques are no longer widely accepted throughout Italy.

## GETTING AROUND

What about Italian transportation? My suggestion is to hop on buses, trains, and planes for the longest stretches, then rent a car for the countryside and the hinterlands, which are spectacular. You definitely want to enjoy these areas at your own pace. But not having a car in the cities will save you the headache of figuring out where you can park it.

**By Train.** To get around within Italy, you'll want to take trains as much as you can, especially when traveling between the larger cities.

Check raileurope.com for schedules, and book your train tickets a few days in advance to be sure you secure a seat.

You can sleep on the train in a compartment that has two to four berths, called *cuccette*. Unless you specify that you want the compartment all to yourself and are willing to pay for that, you will have to share it with a stranger.

**By Bus.** An important rule to follow when it comes to public transit is that you must validate your ticket when you board a bus. If you're willing to learn how the bus system works, you can buy a number of prepaid bus tickets so that you can hop on the bus anytime to get wherever you want to go. You need to validate your ticket through a little clock box near the driver when you enter the bus. Make sure you put that ticket through the machine—if you forget or don't punch it, the driver might fine you more than $100, so be careful! By the way, the same thing applies on a subway or train, so be smart.

**By Car.** Traveling by car throughout the entire boot or for the entire time you are in Italy can be quite challenging, but driving does give you the freedom to do whatever you please, at your own pace. You can drive through little towns, participating in festivals, saint's celebrations, and other events that take place throughout the year.

If you are planning to rent a car, be sure to bring your valid driver's license. You can get an international driver's permit through the American Automobile Association; you don't need to be a member of AAA to obtain one.

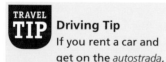

**Driving Tip**
If you rent a car and get on the *autostrada*, the Italian freeway, you will come to a tollbooth every hour or so. Be ready with plenty of change, because on a five-hour drive you can spend as much as $10 going from tollbooth to tollbooth.

**By Taxi or shuttle.** Taxis are expensive. It costs at least $75 to take one from Rome to the airport, versus $15 for a shuttle. Shuttles depart every 20 minutes and will take you to your destination in a short time. If you really want the comfort of a taxi, make sure that you've agreed on a price ahead of time. Write it down, ask the driver if he says okay, and then you have a deal. Don't get in the cab without asking first; that's how many people get themselves into trouble!

Once while I was in the company of American friends in Venice, one of my fellow travelers agreed verbally on a water cab price. But when we arrived at our destination, the driver added another €100 to the bill! I had to intervene, to the great surprise of the Italian cab driver once he realized I was Italian and had heard the initial price.

Get everything in writing. Make sure the price that's written down is what you've both agreed to. Then you can show it to the taxi driver and hop in. Always try to get a receipt. Write down the driver's license number, if you can, so that you can report him if necessary. The laws in Venice are particularly strict, as tourism is their livelihood.

## SHOPPING

Always get receipts for what you buy. Usually Italians won't automatically give them to you, but persist, please, because the police are vigilant and wait for customers outside stores, asking for receipts. If you don't have one, not only will you be fined a lot of euros, but the store could lose its license. The police won't always be there, but I wouldn't chance it.

If you buy any alcohol or olive oil to take back home, make sure that it comes in metal tins, or pack your bottles and goodies well. Tuck these items away in your checked luggage. Don't bring them with you as a carry-on item, because they'll be confiscated and you will be so disappointed. It happened to me with my Don Alfonso *limon* liqueur—what a waste!

If you spend more than $195 on souvenirs, clothing, and gifts in Italy, you can get back the VAT (Valued Added Tax) that you've been charged.

 Travel light, bringing with you only the essentials. You're going to buy lots of stuff anyway when you get to Italy, so it's better to come light and leave heavier.

## SEASONAL NOTES

Around August 14 and 15, Italians are on the move for the national holiday of *Ferragosto* (Assumption Day) and the beginning of their traditional vacation time. This is probably the worst possible time to visit any major city. Prices triple, restaurants prepare food for the masses, and you risk being smothered by overbearing waves of tourists while also suffering from atrocious heat (unless you're heading toward the beach). My advice is to wait until after August 20 to visit the big cities, or to go in May or, at the latest, June. This way you'll find the best deals and receive the best care so that you can enjoy a relaxed visit.

My suggestion is to *not* visit Rome in July or August, as those are the hottest months of the year and traveling will be less comfortable. I recommend the months of May or September, when the sweet Mediterranean climate is perfect!

## STAYING SAFE

Thieves, it's true, are everywhere, and they come in all shapes and sizes. Tourists frequently get targeted, and it can happen as soon as they arrive at the airport. You don't need to be paranoid, but do keep your eyes wide open, especially when you're surrounded by lots of people. Here are a few tips for a stress-free journey:

- Don't wear obviously expensive jewelry or watches. Always try to blend in with other people. If you dress like an affluent tourist, you'll be a target.
- Keep your wallet in your purse, or in a pocket where no one can get to it from behind. Leave your valuables in your hotel in a safe, or make sure they are well hidden where no one else can get to them.
- Ask your hotel concierge if there are any neighborhoods that you should avoid.
- Make photocopies of your documents in case the orig-

inals are lost, or at least carry a copy of your passport.

Trust your instincts. If you smell something fishy, walk away immediately to avoid any aggravation. And be sure to avoid any of these scenarios:

**The Newspaper Trick**— Once in a while at the Rome airport, a group of screaming children will wave a bunch of newspapers in tourists' faces, creating confusion and distracting them so they can grab purses or whatever else they can get their hands on. If this happens to you, keep on walking. Don't get stuck on the idea of how cute these Italian kids are!

**The Mustard Trick**—If you're in a food court, the person next to you might "accidentally" squirt mustard on your shirt, then apologize and try to clean it off. Beware! He may have a partner who will steal your carry-on. Always keep your bag between your legs or secure it to yourself with a strap.

**The Bracelet Scheme**— When you are feeling totally confused, someone might approach you with advice on interesting things to see in the city. You won't even realize that he has wrapped a bracelet around your wrist with a double knot, so that you can't take it off. Then he'll scream that you stole it and must pay for it. Some people feel so distressed by this situation that they end up paying a handful of euros just to make the person to go away.

**The Drinking Rip-off**—This takes advantage of women traveling alone or in pairs. You might meet a couple of guys at a nightclub or pub, and you feel like the most beautiful women in the world because these good-looking men have invited you to have drinks with them. They'll ask you to sit with them in a secluded part of the club, and they'll order round after round of alcohol. Then you'll have a rude awakening when the highly inflated bill arrives. The men will walk away, saying they need to go to the bathroom, and the waiter (he's part of the scam) will tell you that at that time of night they don't take credit cards. The bouncer will ask you to pay up and leave, or else. The moral: do not have drinks with strangers. If you do meet someone, make sure they're the ones to pay first.

Although I've shared with you here a few things that sometimes happen to very naïve travelers, you needn't be overly concerned. Italians are not out to rip you off. Things can happen anywhere in any country to anyone, so just stay alert and you'll be just fine.

 As you get ready for your trip to Italy, be sure to visit our special website: WhereDidTheyFilmThatItaly. com for even more travel information and touring ideas. Plus, you'll find info on my music, great products to buy, and much more!

## TRAVEL AIDS

Electricity operates on different voltages and frequencies in Italy than in the United States (220 volts alternating at 50 cycles per second in Italy, compared to 110 volts at 60 cycles in the U.S.). The electrical sockets are different, too. You'll want to make sure to use the right power converters and plug adapters for your laptop or any other personal electronics. Ask at your local electronics store for the correct converter for Italy. This is about your safety and the safety of your expensive electronics. If you're planning to spend quite a bit of time in Italy, you may want to consider carrying a power strip (with a surge protector) so you can charge multiple devices at once.

*Italian Type L power plugs and sockets.*

 **TRAVEL TIP** The city of Rome has an abundance of historical sites to see, and Bus 64 will take you through the entire city—from the Colosseum to the Forum to the Pantheon—very inexpensively (around €1.50). But be aware that because this is the most popular bus for tourists, it's also targeted by pickpockets. They often work in teams of three or four, grabbing cameras, wallets, or other valuables. Keep close tabs on all your possessions and don't get distracted.

## TELEPHONE NUMBERS

### Emergency Numbers

The most essential phone number you need to know in Italy is 112. This is the universal European emergency number, equivalent to 911 in the United States. 112 will connect you directly to an emergency operator who can dispatch police, fire, and ambulance services. 112 operators speak English as well as Italian, French, and German.

In addition to the pan-European 112 emergency number, there are also some emergency numbers specific to Italy:

| | |
|---|---|
| 112 | General emergency/ Carabinieri |
| 113 | Regular police |
| 115 | Fire services |
| 116 | Car breakdown roadside assistance |
| 118 | Ambulance |
| 12 | Directory assistance |

### Italian area codes and phone number format

You must ALWAYS dial the full phone number, including the area code, to make a phone call in Italy, even when you're calling a number in the same city. Italian phone numbers usually start with a 0, and you must include the 0 when dialing to make a call. Italian phone numbers have between 6 to 11 digits, and most phone numbers are 9 or 10 digits long.

Italian phone numbers are typically written with spaces between the area code, prefix, and number, rather than dashes, e.g. 06 1234 5678.

### Calling Italy from the United States

To reach an Italian phone number from the United States, first dial the U.S. international direct dialing code, 011, plus the country code for Italy, 39, and then the area code and number. For example, to dial a number in Rome from the U.S.:
011 39 06 1234 5678.

Italian phone numbers throughout this book are written in standard international format, e.g. +39 06 1234 5678.

### Calling the United States from Italy

To reach an American number from Italy, first dial the Italian international direct dialing code, 00, plus the country code for the United States, and then the area code and number. For example, to dial a number in Los Angeles from Italy: 00-1-213-555-1234.

# 5

# Milan, Lake Como, and Verona— and the magic of love

*"The real voyage of discovery consists not in seeking new landscapes but in having new eyes."* —MARCEL PROUST

## MILAN

We start our tour near the top of Italy's boot, in the city of Milan—or Milano, as we Italians call it. Visiting Milan is like stepping into the core of fashion, with a unique classic approach. Considered throughout the world to be the capital of all things beautiful, Milan is a center of business and growth as well as being a mecca of design and pure elegance—and we haven't even touched on the food and wine! This city has some of the best chefs in the world, enticing you at every turn with their delicious creations and rich recipes.

Milan is a beautiful city, one of the most breathtaking in Europe in my opinion, with sophisticated architecture and historic art and monuments. When in my mind I place myself back in the heart of this splendid city, I think about the fact that Leonardo da Vinci himself walked this same path,

*The second largest church in Italy, the Milan Cathedral took nearly 600 years to build.*

**MOVIES**

- I Am Love
- A Month by the Lake
- Star Wars:
    Attack of the Clones
- Casino Royale
- Ocean's Twelve
- Letters to Juliet

**TRAVEL TIP** The Milan Tourist Office at 1 Piazza Castella is a wealth of information about the city, how to get around, ticket prices, and itineraries (+39 02 77404343; www.visitamilano.it/turismo_en). It's open weekdays 9 am to 6 pm, Saturday 9 am to 1:30 pm and 2 to 6 pm, Sunday and holidays 9 am to 1:30 pm and 2 to 5 pm. There's also an information booth at the Centrale train station.

I advise you to get the Milano Card, which will give you free transport and discounts for many of the city's best sights and more than 30 restaurants. It costs €9.50 for 24 hours or €10 for 72 hours, and can be purchased online at www.milanocard.it, or at the airport or tourist office. (Be sure to get it *before* you arrive at a restaurant or attraction where you plan to use it.)

probably with the same sense of discovery.

## History and Art

One of the emblems of this industrialized yet historic city is the magnificent **Milan Cathedral**—the Duomo di Milano. This immense, breathtaking Gothic structure in the heart of the city represents the splendor of Milan. Built over a period of six centuries beginning in 1386, it can actually accommodate 40,000 people. The Duomo has 3,500 statues and 135 spires—and an elevator to take you up to the roof so you can walk among them. When you reach the rooftop and take in the 360-degree panorama of the city, a sense of magic and freedom fills your heart. It feels as if you're about to open your wings and fly over the city!

• Open daily from 7 am to 7 pm; for more details, go to duomomilano.it.

When visitors come to Milan, they of course also want to see da Vinci's stunning 15th-century mural *The Last Supper. The Last Supper* is at the refectory of Santa Maria della Grazie church, at the western edge of central Milan (closed Mondays). Making advance reservations to see this incredible work of art is an absolute must! You won't be able to just buy a ticket and walk in. But you can organize your trip and buy tickets in advance by going to this informative website: www.tickitaly.com/tickets/last-supper-tickets.php.

Tickets to view Leonardo da Vinci's *Last Supper* go on sale three months in advance and are quickly sold out. Don't be unprepared as it's very hard

to get tickets on the spot or to make reservation on the same day. My suggestion to you is to book tickets way in advance, as

**INSIDER TIP** Here's a tip, from my uncle Michele Arena, who lives in Milan. I've mentioned the view from the roof of the Duomo, but check this out: you can have what's almost a 3D experience of the Duomo itself from the rooftop cafés in La Rinascente department store. As you enjoy a delicious Italian pastry or a glass of wine, it will almost feel as if you're seated amidst the cathedral spires. Similar to Harrods in London, the Rinascente is open daily until midnight. It's in Piazza Duomo, with entrances also on Via Santa Radegonda and Via San Raffaele.

*Da Vinci's magnificent Last Supper is perhaps the most famous painting in history.*

*For more than 200 years, Italy's greatest operatic artists have performed in the imposing La Scala opera house.*

soon as you book your flights to Italy and plan to visit this extraordinary place!

You can also book your tickets by telephone at +39 0571 981064, from Monday to Friday from 8:00 am until 6:30 pm, Italian time. Operators speak English. The call center is usually very busy, but you may want to try it, as you may have more choices for available days/times than the ones listed on the website. You can also book guided tours in English.

You are only allowed about 15 minutes to view this masterpiece, which captures the dramatic moment at which Jesus reveals that one of his disciples will betray him. It's wonderful to hear the sound of silence as people (about 15 at a time) stare at the painting in awe and almost a posture of prayer—just as I do each time I come here. Da Vinci was a genius and a man of great heart and vision. Seeing his majestic creation is such a powerful experience that you almost feel you are seated at that

table. You can't help but think how incredible it is that such a delicate but powerful piece of history has survived explosions, wars, erosions, and horrible environmental conditions.

Another "must" for me is a visit to La Scala, the most prestigious opera house in the world! La Scala was inaugurated in 1778 as the New Royal-

Ducal Theatre at La Scala, and since then famous singers and dancers from all over the world have graced its golden stage or trained at its Academy. Buy a ticket for the next big production or at least visit the stunning museum, with its priceless art, costumes, musical instruments, and memorabilia from hundreds of year of opera

## When to Visit

Milan gets very cold in winter, so to have the most perfect experience, I recommend that you come in May or perhaps early September. These months are neither cold nor extremely hot. Between April and May the temperature is usually in the 60s or 70s, so it's ideal. In June the thermometer climbs to the 80s and near-90s. If you don't mind the heat, this can be a good time to visit, because many people leave Milan for their vacations and the city is less crowded. But I did warn you, it gets hot!

Unless you love cold weather, I wouldn't recommend visiting in winter. You'll have a hard time walking through the streets and enjoying sites such as the rooftop of the Duomo. Still, Milan is a great place to enjoy the perfect Christmas. The city becomes wonderfully festive, and the shops are draped in holiday finery and stay open late. On December 7, the feast of San Ambroio—the city's patron saint—is celebrated with a huge market in the streets around Piazza Sant'Ambrogio.

history (open 9 am to 12:30 pm and 1:30 to 5:30 pm daily). • Piazza della Scala, just north of Piazza Duomo (where the main box office is located); website teatroallascala.org/en/, phone +39 02 88791.

You can even take a look behind the scenes at the Ansaldo Workshops with guided tours of the old steel plants where La Scala's sets and costumes are designed and created. Tours in English are offered Tuesday and Thursday at 3 pm (must be booked in advance). • Via Bergognone 34, phone +39 02 43353521.

## On the Water in Milan

Milan's *navigli* are ancient man-made canals (something like those in Venice) once used for transportation and irrigation. Now many artists and craftsmen live in what is known as the Navigli district,

southwest of the city's historic center, and in May a giant open-air art show takes place along the banks of the Naviglio Grande. There's also an antiques market here on the last Sunday of every month except July.

Touring this neighborhood by boat is a remarkable experience. One of the most popular trips is called Naviglio Grande Milano—the Conche (pronounced "konka"). The ride lasts about an hour and focuses on the area's history and culture, from the centuries-old Lavandal clothes-washing alley to the 14th-century church of St. Christopher. I enjoyed the trip tremendously, in part because I learned so many new things about Milan's history. (I was born and raised in Italy, but you can never know enough about your own country!) Afterward, you can

explore the little shops and street stalls along the banks. To learn more about the canals, visit naviglilive.it (you can use Google Translate for an English version). Make tour reservations online at ecomm. autostradale.it or call +39 02 36565694 Monday through Friday, 10 am to 1 pm and 2:30 to 5 pm local time..

If you have children (or even if you don't), in summer it's fun to take a break at Idroscalo Lake (www.idroscalo.info). Just a few miles east of the city near Linate Airport, the 1 1/2-mile-long man-made lake is where the locals go for a day at the beach. You'll find boats of all sorts, windsurfing, waterskiing, bicycles to rent, play equipment, a kiddie pool, and even skateboard ramps. Opened in 1930 as a seaplane base, Idroscalo was used by Mussolini as a landing strip. Right next door is Europark Idroscalo Milano, a theme park with rides and entertainment (lunaeuropark.it; open March–October).

## The Fashion Scene

I think you will find yourself falling in love with Milan's lifestyle and haute-couture fashions, so you must visit the Vittorio Emanuele Galleria. This monumental four-story mall with elegant glass-covered walkways and glass dome was completed in 1877. Here you will find all the greatest brands in the world—and you'll be inspired with every step you take because of the fabulous architecture that

*Glamorous at night, the Naviglio Grande is the center of the artsy Navigli district.*

Built in 1877 and named after the first King of Italy, the Vittorio Emanuele Galleria is the one of the oldest shopping malls in the world.

surrounds you. This is one of my favorite things about the Galleria: its front entrance is where the Duomo is, and its back entrance is where La Scala is. So you can spend an entire day shopping and exploring the magnificent Duomo and then end your day with a spectacular opera performance. Now, that sounds like a lot to cover in one day, but we only live once, right? Live the life you love!

Right inside the Galleria, you'll find several bars. (Remember, a bar in Italy is a place where you can enjoy an espresso or a pastry.) Be aware that these are extremely expensive—you could pay $15 for coffee! There's also a sublime restaurant called **Biffi**, very pricey but worth it. Another posh coffee place is the **Gucci Café**, for coffee and chocolate.

You'll find many more fashion stores at a couple other areas close to the Galleria, **Corso Buenos Aires** and **Via Montenapoleone**. You can find amazing clothing and accessories here, a bit less expensive than at the Galleria though still pretty pricey. And right off Via Montenapoleone is the brand-new **Excelsior** shopping mall.

Milan is a powerhouse of haute couture, where fashions jump from catwalk to clothes rack in a matter of weeks. Here's the trick: the best clothing stores and boutiques are all located in one square. Via della Spiga, Via Manzoni, Via Sant'Andrea, and Via Montenapoleone create something the Milanese call the "**Rectangle of Gold**." This area offers the very best, and sometimes you can find great deals. On a recent trip I found an Armani jacket fresh off the runway at a very low price because it was a sample. Designer stores include Armani, Chanel, Missoni, Prada, and Versace. I do have to warn you that about 85% of the items sold in these stores are priced above €500—and I'm only talking about the shoes! But you never know, you might just find that deal you can't pass up.

I have to confess that I'm a hopeless shopaholic. I try to find unique things in the places I visit, and I've learned to go where the locals go. In Milan I followed a woman who was carrying many fashion bags and still managing to talk on her cell phone. I ended up in **Corso Porta Ticinese**, the perfect place when it comes to shopping. Vibrant with lots of young people, this area is very close to Via Torino, a little closer to the center of the fashion district, with both big-name shops and intimate boutiques filled with fabulous clothing and colorful bags, shoes, and belts. I noticed the sophistication of women wearing extremely high heels and suits that were almost seductive, with perfect makeup and hair, as if they'd stepped out of a fashion magazine. For the people of Milan, casual is what we'd consider very elegant!

Shops here are geared toward the American market with brands such as Lee, Quiksilver, and Energy. But wait! Did I mention Italian shoes? The shoes are more unique than what you can find in the main shopping houses and often are quite well priced. What better souvenir than a pair of Italian shoes?

Of course, when you spend all day on your feet shopping, you'll probably want to take a break for a special lunch. I have the perfect place for you. A favorite spot of many Mil-

## ON LOCATION MILAN

MOVIE *I Am Love*
RELEASE 2009
DIRECTOR **Luca Guadagnino**
CAST **Tilda Swinton, Pippo Delbono,**
  **Edoardo Gabbriellini**

In this Italian-made film, Emma (Swinton) has left Russia to become the wife of Tancredi Recchi (Delbono), a member of a powerful Milanese industrial family. She is now the respected mother of three. But Emma, although not unhappy, feels confusingly unfulfilled.

*The music for the movie was written by Pulitzer Prize-winning composer John Adams.*

One day Antonio (Gabbriellini), a talented chef and her son's friend and partner, makes her fall in love with him through his seductive food. The two enter into a passionate love affair, with dangerous consequences.

When I watched this film for the first time, I was taken by it in every sense. The hot and steamy passion between the leading lady and her young lover is unforgettable. And because I'm a musician, the score by composer John Adams had me pulsing along with the movie from the very start. It all happens in a gorgeous house framed by the beautiful colors of Milan, accompanied by the flavors of the local food and a great sense of style. By the way, this is definitely not a chick flick—men should see it, too.

*For her role in* I Am Love, *Tilda Swinton learned both Italian and Russian—neither of which she spoke before getting the part.*

Almost the entire movie was shot in **Villa Necchi Campiglio**, a 1930s mansion in the heart of Milan that was designed by architect Piero Portaluppi. The leading actress—who was also one of the producers—said she thought the villa was ideal for *I Am Love* because it was part palace, part museum, and part prison. For more information about the villa, go to casemuseomilano.it/en/. For an organized tour, you can contact Stephania Rossi at Museo Poldi Pezzoli (phone +39 02 45473813; rossi@museopoldipezzolo.it).

anese business people is **Bar Della Crocetta**, where a normal sandwich becomes an art form. They offer more than 100 wonderful sandwich ingredients—from wild venison to prosciutto to basil-flavored goat cheese or marinated artichokes—to be squeezed between thin pieces of their own secret-recipe grilled bread.• Bar della Crocetta, Corso di Porta Romana, 67, 20122, Milan, +39 02 545 0228.

And if you want something other than a *panino*, behind La Rinascente department store at Piazza Duomo is **Panzerotti Luini**, famous for its *panzerotti*—rounds of dough stuffed with tomato and mozzarella, then folded and fried. Just one thing, you might want to eat later in the afternoon and not right at lunchtime, because these two places are so popular that you'll have to wait forever for a table unless you're there early (say 11 am).

## Special Events

There's always something happening in Milan! These are some of my favorite events:

• **Fiore e Sapori** ("Flowers and Flavors") in April through October is a time to savor food prepared by talented local chefs throughout the city. Special menus and delicious new dishes are created to entice tourists and locals to participate in the life of slow food, enjoying meals in settings where conversation and the exchange of ideas is encouraged. For more infor-

mation visit naviogliogrande. mi.it/fiori-sapori.

• **Milan Fashion Week** for women takes place in late February, and if you are like me and love fashion, you'll be very excited by this divine celebration of color and high-end design. Check this website for information: cameramoda.it/en. Fashion Week for men is in January, and Vogue Fashion's Night Out is in September.

It is not an easy thing to have access to Milan Fashion Week, unless you are a celebrity or involved in the fashion industry (or you claim to be a cousin of Dolce or Gabbana … you can always try!). But one of the insiders of Fashion Week in Milan has told me about a wonderful website that will allow you to check the availability and prices of tickets, and purchase them if available. For details visit providingtickets.com/request-fashion-week-tickets.

• **Milan Men's Fashion Week**, in late January, is not the most important event in Milan's fashion calendar, but it does bring some of the world's best-looking men to the city. Shows, events, special presentations and catwalks take place all over town. For details, visit cameramoda.it/en.

• **Milano Food Week**, held annually in May or June, is when top chefs and Italian food companies present a glorious feast of food and wine. At events all over the city you can try practically

everything on the map when it comes to Italian guilty food pleasures. There are cooking classes and demonstrations, art exhibits, and all sorts of

## Romina's Hotel Pick

**PARK HYATT MILAN**
To experience pure diamond service and luxury while you are in Milan, stay at this hotel. Located next to the Vittorio Emanuele Galleria in the heart of the city, the classical-style Park Hyatt offers the very best of what you expect from a five-star hotel. The hospitality of the staff is outstanding, and the rooms and suites are so comfortable and elegant that you could literally cocoon yourself. (My favorite is the Imperial Suite, with its precious art objects and paintings— perfect for a luxurious Italian honeymoon!) But since the hotel is next to the Galleria, why not shop during the day and then come back to get ready before heading off to dinner and the opera? See—you have the perfect day planned. Daily rates: around €450 to €600, depending on the season. *Via Tommaso Grossi, 1 20121 Milan* **Web** *milan.park.hyatt.com* **Phone** *+39 02 8821 1234;* *(800) 633-7313 in the U.S.*

tastings, many of them free and open to the public. You can join the Milano Food Lovers community at milanofoodweek.it to take part in special tastings (joining is free).

- **Mercato dei Fiori**, or Flower Fair, takes place in April along the Naviglio Grande. This is the most colorful event in Italy! Over 200 nurseries and horticultural schools from all around Italy come together to create a spectacular splash of color along the canal. For more information visit navigliogrande.mi.it or call +39 02 89409971.
- **La Notte Bianca**, which takes place all over Milan in mid-June. In Italian, a "white night" is a sleepless night. For one night each year, bars, restaurants, shops, cinemas stay open from early evening to 6 am. For details see the Milan city website, comune.milano.it.
- **Milano d'Estate**, or Summer in Milan, takes place between June and August on the grounds of the magnificent and historic Castello Sforzesco. Through the summer, open-air concerts by major international music stars entertain those unfortunate *milanesi* who can't leave the city in the heat of the summer. For more information and this year's schedule, visit visitamilano.it.
- **La Scala Opening Night**: On December 7 of every year, the famous La Scala Theatre has its glorious Opening Night! La Piazza della Scala is filled with splendid gowns and feather boas and black ties, and the great and the good assemble for La Scala's first night of the season. This is a must! Teatro alla Scala, Via Filodrammatici 2, 20121 Milano, +39 02 88791, teatroallascala.org/en.

## Getting to Milan

Transportation to and within Milan is very well organized so you needn't feel stressed about traveling here. This is probably one of the best-planned cities in Europe.

Shuttle buses found outside the train station run directly to Milan's two airports (be sure to get on the right bus—for either Malpensa or Linate airport). Milan's metro system connects the train station with the historic city center and other parts of Milan. Check the Milan Transportation Map (you'll find them throughout the stations) for more information about the metro and airport transportation.

**Arriving by air**—Italy's largest international airports are in Milan and Rome, 358 miles to the south, so travelers can get between the two cities quickly. Milan has two airports: the larger Milan Malpensa, with many international flights, and the smaller Milan Linate, with flights mainly from other parts of Italy and Europe. Buses connect both airports with Milan's central train station.

**Arriving by train**—Frequent trains run between Rome's Termini and Milan's Centrale stations. A few fast trains also leave from the Tiburtina station in Rome. Trains depart daily from early morning until about 11 pm. There is also an overnight train with sleeping facilities that currently leaves Rome about 11 pm and arrives in Milan about 7 am.

Fast Eurostar Altovelocita (ESA) trains make the trip from

*The Milan Central Station is one of the main transport hubs of northern Italy.*

Rome to Milan in as little as 3 1/2 hours, although some take 4 hours. Eurostar (ES) and Intercity (IC) trains take from 5 to 6 1/2 hours. The fastest ESA trains cost almost double what the IC trains cost.

Be sure to reserve your seat ahead of time. To check schedules and purchase tickets, go to the Trenitalia website, trenitalia.com (or search "Trenitalia in English" for a translation). Travelers from the U.S. may find it convenient to buy their train tickets ahead of time through selectitaly.com.

*The Como-Brunante Funicular is steep, but modern, comfortable, and safe.*

## LAKE COMO

From Milan, it's just an hour's drive north to the splendidly picturesque high-end resort area of Lake Como. There is also easy access by train service connecting the two points.

My favorite little Lake Como town is called **Varenna**, nestled among green hills on the lake's eastern shore with a group of ancient and elegant towns, including **Bellagio** and **Nebbia**—each one amazing and scenic in its own way. Be

prepared to do lots of walking here, because there are many stairs and some magnificent hikes. Varenna lies about 37 miles north of Milan and 12 miles northwest of **Lecco** in the Lombardy region. This town is known as "the pearl of Lake Como," and you'll see why when you experience the stunning views of the lake and mountains. To top things off, Varenna is home to Italy's shortest river, the 820-foot-long Fiumelatte.

The town of **Como** is a gateway to the lake at its southwest tip. You'll get a terrific view of the area on a **funicular railway** that climbs from Como to the village of Brunate, a ride of only 7 minutes. The rail line has been in operation since 1894. Trains operate from 6 am to 10:30 pm, and to midnight on Saturdays and in summer. I don't suggest this in the off-season, as a lot

of the fun things to do at the top of the hill are closed then. This spot is popular with locals but not so widely known by tourists. Warning: if you're afraid of heights, skip this ride, as it's really steep! • Website funicolarecomo.it, phone +39 031 303608; €5.25 round trip.

For still more spectacular views, you might want to take the **C20 bus** between Como and Argegno. It's about a 40-minute ride, winding high above the lake.

Lake Como is known for its elegant villas, and one of the most famous is **Villa del Balbianello** on the west side, across the lake from Bellagio. Built in the late 18th century, the villa is an Italian Trust site—learn more at fondoambiente.it—and has been featured in a number of movies (see page 32). To get there, take the ferry to Lenno, then catch the water shuttle to the Lecco landing

*The beautiful Villa del Balbianello has been featured in films as varied as* A Month by the Lake *and* Casino Royale.

stage. Wear comfortable shoes; it's an uphill climb of more than half a mile. The entrance fee gives you access to the terraced garden, a fantasyland where trees are shaped like chandeliers and your path is bordered by ancient statues and wisteria vines. The view of the lake is absolutely stunning. For an additional fee you can have a guided tour of the villa itself, in either English or Italian. You'll have to purchase a camera pass to take photos inside, or you can buy picture books or postcards in the tiny gift shop. • Open mid-March to mid-November, 10 am to 6 pm (closed Monday and Wednesday); Via Comoedia 5, Lenno; phone +39 0344 56110.

Villa del Balbianello is a popular wedding venue. Who knows, it could be the perfect romantic backdrop for your own Italian wedding! To explore the possibilities, visit villabalbianello.com; or contact Lake Como wedding planner Sabina Domenici (foreveramoreweddings.com; phone +39 347 3503290).

## Home of the Rich and Famous

Lake Como has been home to numerous celebrities. Actor George Clooney has owned the 18th-century lakeside Villa L'Oleandra in Laglio since 2001. British billionaire and entrepreneur Sir Richard Branson owns a large villa that

you can see when you visit Villa del Balbianello. Muse front man Matthew Bellamy and Brazilian soccer star Ronaldinho both have homes here, and the late fashion designer Gianni Versace resided at the Villa Le Fontanell in Moltrasio.

Movie stars and other famous folks come here because they are pulled into a world of enchantment and repose, a glamorous "simple" life where they are surrounded by natural beauty in a tranquil environment away from traffic, hubbub, and the paparazzi. Lake Como practically defines the word "glamour." Shop in Bellagio (yes, this town was the inspiration for the Las Vegas hotel) or visit Villa del Balbaniello or Villa D'Este and you'll be struck by the dazzling elegance of the surroundings. Stroll Bellagio's lavish gardens and stop in the prestigious 19th-century Grand Hotel Villa Serbelloni, with its amazing artwork.

## GRAND HOTEL VILLA SERBELLONI

*Via Roma 1*
*22021 Bellagio*
**Website:** *villaserbelloni.com*
**Phone:** *+39 031 950216*

## Around the Lake

It's great fun to **tour the lake by motorboat**. You can rent a private motorboat to visit the towns of Bellagio, Varenna, and Menaggio, or hop on a ferry or hydrofoil). For timetables, phone +39 800 551801 or +39 031 579211 or visit www. navigazionelaghi.it/eng.

Here are my suggestions for a few more unique Lake Como experiences:

- Fly over the lake in a **seaplane**, then land on the water for a quick swim!

- Visit the adorable town of **Mezzagra**, where Mussolini and his mistress were executed. (I know, the event was less than adorable, but this place attracts tourists from all over the world.) Mezzagra is on the western branch of the lake about 12 miles from Como.

- In Como, tour the **silk museum**, Museo Didattico della Seta, and find out why this is "the city of silk." • Via Castelnuovo 9, website museosetacomo.com, phone +39 031 303180; open Tuesday–Friday, 9 am to noon and 3 to 6 pm; admission €10.

- In Bellagio, take in one of the **summer concerts** organized by the Rockefeller Foundation Center in conjunction with the Capuchin church on its grounds.

### Take Note!

Everything that is music and romance attracts me! As I was sailing on Lake Como, I thought about the fact that this setting has inspired several major composers. Bellini composed *Norma* at the lake, and this is where Verdi created Act II of *La Traviata*. Soprano Giuditta Pasta, the Maria Callas of her day, was the favorite choice to sing these notes. And here I was, enjoying the lyrical setting of her famous villa, reborn in 2010 as the luxury resort **CastaDiva**. The villa is just north of Como at Blevio (castadivaresort.com).

Singers and composers alike have been captivated by **Villa Melzi** at Bellagio. Liszt wrote his *Dante Sonata* on these shores, supposedly inspired by a statue of Dante and Beatrice at Villa Melzi. The villa's vast gardens are open daily, April through October, from 9:30 am to 6:30 pm (giardinidivilla melzi.it; phone +39 339 4573838).

*Boats on Lake Como.*

## A Perfect Day at Lake Como

» Wake up in the early morning for a kayaking trip near Bellagio. **Bellagio Water Sports** will make the arrangements for you (bellagiowatersports.com, phone +39 340 394375).

» Walk through the cobbled alleyways of Bellagio and take in the lake views from the graceful gardens of **Villa Melzi**. Pause for a delicious fish lunch at the rustic **Silvio** restaurant (Via Carcano 12, phone +39 31 950322; free shuttle from Bellagio).

» Boat across to Tremezzo at the lushest part of the lake. Have dinner in Cernobbio, either beneath the wisteria pergola of **Trattoria del Glicine** (Via Carcano 1, phone +39 031 511332) or at **Il Gatto Nero**, one of George Clooney's favorite dining spots (Via Monte Santo 69, phone +39 031 512042).

*A view of the gorgeous gardens at the Villa Melzi.*

## ON LOCATION LAKE COMO

Several locations around Lake Como were used for the filming of the 1995 romantic comedy *A Month by the Lake*, starring Vanessa Redgrave and Uma Thurman and directed by John Irvin. One of them was the spectacular **Villa del Balbianello**, a former Franciscan monastery set right on the water at Lenno (see page 29). This villa was also seen in George Lucas' 2002 film *Star Wars: Attack of the Clones*, serving as the secret hideaway where Anakin Skywalker (Hayden Christensen) and Padmé Amidala (Natalie Portman) were married.

Villa del Balbianello was also where Daniel Craig's James Bond recuperated in the 2006 hit movie *Casino Royale*, directed by Martin Campbell. (The end of *Casino Royale*, when Bond shoots Mr. White, was filmed at the breathtaking Villa La Gaeta, in San Siro.)

And because we are in Lake Como and George Clooney has a home here, we must talk about *Ocean's Twelve*, starring Clooney, Julia Roberts, Brad Pitt, and Matt Damon. The 2004 movie, directed by Steven Soderbergh, was filmed at the chic **Villa Erba** (on the southwest shore in Cernobbio), representing the mansion of Baron François Toulour in the movie. A number of other movies have been shot at this location. You can book a tour or even organize a splendid wedding or other event at the villa. *Villa Erba, Largo Luchino Visconti 4, Cernobbio; phone +39 031 3491.*

In addition to all this, Gwen Stefani shot the video for her song "Cool" around the lake. Track down her video, and you'll fall in love with Lake Como just by watching it. The song is a great plus!

## Getting to Lake Como

Once you've arrived in Milan, you have a number of options for getting to the lake. The town of **Como** is on the Switzerland-to-Milan train line, and there's direct service from Milan. From Malpensa International Airport, you can take the express train to **Saronno** (where that delicious Amaretto di Saronno liqueur comes from) and change to a Como train. If you arrive in Milan by air, you can take a shuttle bus to Milan Central Station to get a train to Como (approximately 40 minutes).

But I suggest that you rent a car—it's such a picturesque drive from Milan to Lake Como that you won't want to miss it! On your way out of Milan, you can stop at the wonderful old **Peck Deli** for an out-of-this-world risotto or coffee and a pastry. • Via Spadari 9, phone +39 02 8023161.

Lake Como lies between Milan and Switzerland, so you can imagine the incredible panorama that will surround you as you navigate the narrow roads. Just watch out for those

**Romina's Hotel Picks**

### CASA MARA

Right on the lake in the center of Varenna, Casa Mara occupies the first floor of a lovely typical Varenna villa. It has two bedrooms, a spacious living room, a very modern bathroom (with shower and washing machine), a useful kitchen, and an amazing-view balcony. The Casa usually books for Saturday-to-Saturday stays, and it is almost always fully booked—so make your reservation ASAP. You can book directly with the villa (reservations@ homeinvarenna.com) or through FlipKey.com or HomeAway.co.uk. Weekly rates: €650 to €800.
*Via Pirelli 6*
*Varenna*

### RELAIS REGINA TEODOLINDA

This hotel in the peaceful little town of Laglio is another extraordinary place to be pampered while you explore Lake Como. The 19th-century residence of a noble family from Milan, it has been transformed into a six-suite hotel. Daily rates: €150 to €520.
*Via Vecchia Regina 58*
*22010 Laglio*
**Web** *villareginateodolinda. com*
**Phone** *+39 031 400031*

### VILLA D'ESTE

This breathtaking hotel made me feel like royalty. Built in the 16th century as a princely summer residence, the 152-room luxury hotel is on the lake's southwestern arm at Cernobbio. You can book a suite in the main hotel building or really splurge and choose one of the private villas. (I suggest Villa Cima, which is spectacular.) The epitome of elegance, Villa d'Este features 25 acres of Renaissance-style gardens. Only a few minutes away is Italy's oldest golf club. Daily rates: €425 to €1,370.
*Via Regina 40*
*22012 Cernobbio*
**Web** *villadeste.com*
**Phone** *+39 031 3481*

And if money is no object, here are three world-class five-star hotels:

### HOTEL BELVEDERE
*Via Valassina 31*
*22021 Bellagio*
**Web** *belvederebellagio. com*
**Phone** *+39 031 950410*

### HOTEL DU LAC
*Piazza Mazzini 32*
*22021 Bellagio*
**Web** *bellagiohoteldulac. com*
**Phone** *+39 031 950320*

### GRAND HOTEL VILLA SERBELLONI
*Via Roma 1*
*22021 Bellagio*
**Web** *villaserbelloni.com*
**Phone** *+39 031 950216*

crazy Italian drivers (sorry, fellow Italians), and don't let your attention be diverted by that enormous blue body of water stretching out before you with its elegant yachts and charming villas.

**From Milan to Varenna by train**—From Malpensa International Airport, take a shuttle bus to Milano Centrale (Central Milan railway station); Malpensa Shuttle is one of many bus companies offering service. From Linate Airport, Starfly Shuttle is among the buses you can take to the railway station. Orio Shuttle operates between Orio al Serio Airport and the train railway station.

From Milano Centrale, take the train to Tirano and get off at Varenna-Esino railway station (the stops are Monza, Lecco, Varenna-Esino). The trip takes slightly more than an hour. You can book tickets at trenoitalia.it.

**From Milan to Varenna by road**—I recommend using Google Maps or a satellite navigator. From Malpensa International Airport, take the A336 to the A8 toward Milan, then the A4 toward Venice. Take exit SP5 and head toward Lecco on the SS36; turn off this autostrada to Varenna and Mandello. Total distance: approximately 66 miles.

From Linate Airport, take the A1 toward Monza, then the A4 West; then join the SS36 and turn off the autostrada to Varenna and Mandello. Total distance: about 49 miles.

From Orio al Serio Airport, take the SS342 Northwest toward Lecco. Join the SS36 and turn off to Varenna and Mandello. Total distance: about 34 miles.

## VERONA

After Lake Como, we can proceed to the Dolomites—but not before making a stop in the perfect midpoint between the two locations, the romantic city of Verona. Several trains go directly to Verona from Milan and Venice ($25 to $45 one way, raileurope.com).

Besides being known for Shakespeare's dramatic love story of *Romeo and Juliet*, this

*Built in the first century AD, the Verona Arena is one of the best preserved structures of Roman times and is still in operation.*

*Piazza delle Erbe in the heart of Verona.*

incredible city has a splendid ancient amphitheater that's very similar to the Coliseum in Rome. Dating from AD 30, the **Verona Arena** (Arena di Verona) is now one of the most important venues in Italy for summertime operas and classical concerts. That makes summer the best time to visit Verona, so you can hear incredible music under the stars, surrounded by powerful history. • Arena.it/en, phone +39 045 8005151; seats from €21 (bring a cushion if you buy the cheapest ticket, as these seats aren't comfortable for lengthy sitting).

Recently the Arena opened a museum in collaboration with Milan's La Scala to showcase the history of opera, artists who have graced this stage, costumes, original scores— even handwritten letters by Puccini and Verdi. • Via

Massalongo 7, website www. arenamuseopera.com; open daily 9 am to 7:30 pm April– September, 9:30 am to 7:30 pm (closed Monday) October– March; admission €10, or €5 if you show a ticket for a performance.

The artist in me couldn't control my excitement when I noticed many musicians from the Arena's rehearsal pavilion heading outside for a quick bite. **At Piazza Bra** (*not* dedicated to women's undergarments) you might hear a violinist tuning his instrument right next to you while choirgirls read pentagrams and hum melodies over hot chocolate and Italian cookies.

Elsewhere in Verona, the medieval **Piazza delle Erbe** represents the heart of the city. **Torre dei Lamberti** here is one of the two remaining towers of the **Palazzo del Comune**, the

onetime city hall. The tower dates back to the 12th century and was restored in the mid-15th century after being struck by lightning. The very top of the 275-foot structure was added later, and from here you have a truly spectacular view of the city. Take the elevator, or you can climb the more than 350 steps. (I can tell you from personal experience that you need to be in good shape to do so!) • Via della Costa, 1, Piazza delle Erbe; open daily.

Also in Piazza delle Erbe is the **Fresh Market Square**, Verona's version of a farmers' market. Here you can purchase souvenirs, fresh fruits and vegetables, special panini, and the region's delicious scamorza cheese. Why not improvise a romantic picnic? From the piazza, you can stroll **Via Mazzini**, Verona's premier shopping street. Come evening, this area becomes the city's living room, the place where everyone meets.

If you want a coffee break, **Café Turbino** might be exactly what you're looking for. They take coffee to a whole new place, adding flavors such as

*Entrance to the Castelvecchio.*

hazelnut, chocolate orange, chestnut, and ginseng. There's no sign outside with the café's name, just the image of colorful half cups, a flower, and a sun. You'll recognize it! • Via Porta Borsari 15/D, phone +39 045 8032296; coffee from €1.

From Piazza delle Erbe you can go to an elegant garden called **Torre dei Lamberti**, where locals meet to picnic and enjoy the view—highly recommended. • Via della Costa 1, phone +39 045 9273027. Another beautiful public garden in the neighborhood is Giardino Giusti, Via Giardino Giusti 2, +39 045 8034029, and you can get some wonderful refreshments at Cappa Caffé, +39 045 8004516, Piazzetta Brà Molinari 1.

The medieval fortress of **Castelvecchio** ("old castle") is a military monument to Verona's

onetime noble ruling family, the Scaligera. They built the fortress not for protection from outside invaders but to keep them safe during local uprisings. The 14th-century brick castle also contains the city art museum. • **Museo di Castelvecchio**, Corso Castelvecchio 2, 37121 Verona, +39 045 8062611, museodicastelvecchio.comune. verona.it. Open Tuesday– Sunday from 8:30 am to 7:30 pm, Monday from 1:45 to 7:30 pm.

### The Balcony Scene

Of course, in Verona you'll have the opportunity of visiting the **Juliet balcony** described in Shakespeare's play. Though we all know that Juliet is a fictional character, people from around the world come to see and experience this balcony. They can even go inside the ancient

*According to local legend in Verona, this is the balcony on which Juliet was wooed by Romeo.*

rural home that claims to have belonged to the Capulet family, and take pictures from the famous balcony. And guess what? You can actually get married here!

You can't help but envision the two lovers talking to one another as Juliet stands on her balcony, the air scented with roses. And yes, this vine-clad villa is crowded with love's pilgrims. As each would-be Juliet professes her love for the man of her dreams, she looks out over vineyards and swaths of green. Nearby, the tiny Santa Maria Antica Church could serve as a wedding chapel for runaway lovers. And if you walk a short way, you'll find a street called Via Arche Scaligere where Romeo's home is rumored to have been, at No. 4.

*The Palazzo Piccolomini served as the palace of the Capulets in Franco Zeffirelli's 1968 film of Romeo and Juliet.*

## ON LOCATION VERONA

MOVIE *Letters to Juliet*
RELEASE **2010**
DIRECTOR **Gary Winick**
CAST **Amanda Seyfried, Vanessa Redgrave, Franco Nero, Chris Egan, Gael Garcia Bernal**

*Letters to Juliet* has a special meaning for me, not only because the cast includes one of my favorite Italian actors—Franco Nero—but also because this was the final film by director Gary Winick. He died soon after making the movie, a month short of turning 50. His amazing view of Italy and his sensibility can be felt strongly through almost every scene in the movie. The panorama of Verona, the colors, and even the meals on the table make this movie so cozy and dreamy, a must for lovers of romantic films.

*Letters to Juliet* stars the talented Amanda Seyfried as Sophie. During a trip to Italy with her fiancé, Sophie discovers the famous Juliet wall, where people in love hide secret messages so that—almost by a magic spell—they might be together forever and receive help from Juliet in solving their love heartaches. Sophie ends up with more than she has bargained for when she meets the "Juliets"—women who respond each day to the thousands of messages left by hopeless lovers.

I guess whether you're in love or in search of love, Italy is the place of the heart, most of the time!

In *Letters to Juliet*, Sophie enjoys a wonderful strawberry buttermilk Italian gelato. I want to share with you a quick recipe that will allow you to repeat the delicious experience of pure Italian bliss in your very own kitchen!

### Strawberry–Buttermilk Gelato

*Ingredients*
1 cup sugar
1 cup water
2 pints quartered strawberries
1 cup low-fat buttermilk

1. Mix sugar and water thoroughly in a saucepan. Bring to a boil and stir until the sugar dissolves. Pour into a large bowl and place in the refrigerator until cooled completely.

2. Puree the strawberries (you can use any other kind of berry, if you prefer) in a food processor until smooth.

3. Add the strawberry puree to the syrup you have made with sugar and water. Add buttermilk and stir to combine.

4. Pour the mixture into an ice cream mixer and freeze—the result will be so delicious!

Couples from all over follow the old tradition of touching the breast of the Juliet statue in the courtyard to receive eternal love. Visitors write on the walls of the home and stick little love notes into the cracks in the walls, professing their love. This forms the basis of the plot for the movie *Letters to Juliet* (see sidebar). •Via Cappello 23, phone +39 045 8034303; open Tuesday–Sunday 8:30 am to 7:30 pm, Monday 1:30 to 7:30 pm.

### Did You Know?

Despite the fact that Shakespeare's tragedy is set in Verona, none of the location shooting for Franco Zeffirelli's 1968 movie *Romeo and Juliet* actually took place in the city. Instead, the following locations were used:

**Balcony**: the 17th-century Palazzo Borghese, 20 miles south of Rome in Artena

**Church**: church of Saint Peter (San Pietro) in the town of Tuscania, 50 miles northwest of Rome

**Tomb**: also shot in Tuscania

**Palace of the Capulets**: the town of Pienza in Siena province

**Fight scenes**: the lovely town of Gubbio in the region of Umbria

**TRAVEL TIP** The €15 Verona Card, available at locations throughout the city and good for two days, grants you admission to many sights—including Juliet's house (no charge for the balcony), Juliet's tomb, the Arena, Castelvecchio, and other attractions.

## IL SOGNO DI GIUILIETTA (JULIET'S DREAM)

You can actually spend the night in Juliet's courtyard, across from her balcony in a medieval palazzo. This romantic guesthouse, with its Renaissance-looking rooms and canopied beds, is where the stars of *Letters to Juliet* slept. A two-night stay in low season costs from €369 to €3,200, depending on the room. I know it's pricey, but how can you resist?
*Via Cappello 23*
*37121 Verona*
*Web* sognodigiulietta.it
*Phone +39 045 8009932*

## VILLA D'ACQUARONE HISTORICAL RESIDENCES

One of the most beautiful hotels you could find for a perfect Verona vacation is this villa, offering six rooms in the historic home of the dukes of Acquarone. The villa is about 5 miles east of Verona. Daily rates: €200 to €600.
*Via Pasubio, 5*
*37036 San Martino Buon*
*  Albergo*
*Web* villadacquarone.com
*Phone +39 045 990330*

## ROMEO E GIULIETTA

Named for our romantic heroes as they are called by Italians, this hotel in Verona is a great value and very romantic, if a bit more modern than some. Daily rates (double, off-season): about €148.
*Vicolo Tre Marchetti 3*
*37121 Verona*
*Web* giuliettaeromeo.it
*Phone +39 045 8003554*

## CORTE DELLE PIGNE

If you're watching your pocketbook but still want to have that special romantic time, try this quaint French B&B just five minutes from Piazza delle Erbe. Daily rates (double): from €90.
*Via Pigna 6/A*
*37121 Verona*
*Web* cortedellepigne.it
*Phone +39 333 7584141*

Romina's Hotel Picks

# 6

# Let's explore the colder North . . . and James Bond!

*"Your time is limited, so don't waste it living someone else's life. Don't be trapped by dogma—which is living with the results of other people's thinking. Don't let the noise of others' opinions drown out your own inner voice. And most important, have the courage to follow your heart and intuition. They somehow already know what you truly want to become. Everything else is secondary."* —STEVE JOBS

## THE DOLOMITES

The dramatic Dolomites separate Italy from Austria. In fact, this mountain range raises its jagged peaks right at the border, and people in the region speak both German and Italian. Here you can explore luxurious towns such as Cortina D'Ampezzo and San Candido, which might be compared to Colorado's Aspen or Vail—with the difference that these areas of Italy are filled with history. In 2009 UNESCO named the Dolomites a World Heritage Site—something that must be seen!

If I told you that 2 1/2 million years ago these majestic mountains were a coral reef in the ancient Tethys Ocean, would you believe me? It's completely true, though hard to believe when you see how massive they are. Moving closer

*The Dolomites offer some of the most spectacular scenery in all of Europe.*

to recent times, it is sad to realize that during World War I, between 1915 and 1918, the Dolomites were the scene of a horrific chapter of history when Italian and Austrian soldiers battled here in terrible trench warfare. Reminders of that time are apparent in traces of mines and bombs (inactive now, of course), pretty much everywhere you go. It seems incredible that today the Dolomites are the perfect holiday destination for tourists from all around the world, especially skiers.

If you love cold winters, snow, and historic romantic chalets and cabins, then this place has

*The autonomous province of Alto Adige/South Tyrol.*

## MOVIES

For Your Eyes Only
The Pink Panther

*Italian Alpini troops in 1915. In World War I, Italy and Austria-Hungary fought fierce battles in the Dolomites, in one of the toughest environments in the war. Relics of 100-year-old battles can still be found in the mountains.*

your name written all over it. The Dolomites in December and January are the coldest place in all of Italy—not too bad if you are from Minnesota or Alaska! Those who don't ski can spend their days at one of the many resorts, getting a suntan in the snow or relaxing by the fireplace. Summer offers long hikes and bicycle rides, or swimming beneath waterfalls.

The mix of culture and languages here is especially interesting. The Dolomites, part of the autonomous region of Trentino-Alto Adige/South Tyrol, were under the control of Austria until they were annexed by Italy after World War I. The area is actually trilingual, with German, Italian, and Ladin, the ancient local language, all spoken.

## The Pale Mountains

A French geologist by the name of Déodat Gratet de Dolomieu collected and analyzed mineral samples from these mountains in the late eighteenth century, and the range was eventually named for him. But if you are a hopeless romantic (and Italy is definitely the place for romance!), you might want to know about the original name of the mountains, and the legend of a prince who once lived here. This prince had a burning desire to travel to the moon, and by magic his wish was granted. Once there, he met and fell in love with the princess of the moon, and they were married. When the prince began to lose his sight because the moon was so bright, the couple came back to the mountains. But now the

princess began to suffer, pining for the moon's brightness.

As happens in a lot of fairy tales, some gnomes with fantastic powers appeared on the scene. They promised the prince that if they could make their home in his kingdom, they would find a solution for him. They proceeded to weave rays of moonlight into fine gossamer to cover the mountains with pale color so that the princess and prince could be happy together there for the rest of their lives! To this day these peaks are known as the Pale Mountains, or Monti Pallidi.

It sounds like a movie, doesn't it? And when I think about the city of Narni in Umbria—inspiration for the name in C.S. Lewis' *Chronicles of Narnia,* and the movie made from it—it's not difficult to see just how many great stories have come from Italy.

An amazing British painter and illustrator immortalized the pure splendor of this region a century ago. Reginald Farrer was dedicated to traveling in the Dolomites in the summertime and painting the Alpine flowers. If you love botany, you might want to get hold of his book *The Dolomites,* originally published in 1913. His illustrations are so vivid and so rich in detail that you can almost smell the flowers and feel the chilly sparkling mountain air. Nature truly comes alive through the pages of his book.

Farrer wasn't the only artist with ties to these mountains. Renaissance painter Titian

*Da Vinci's most famous painting. Are the Dolomites peeking around that enigmatic smile?*

*Opening ceremonies of the 1956 Winter Olympics, the event that made Cortina d'Ampezzo world famous.*

(Tiziano Vecelli) was born here, near Belluno, around 1490. And according to close friends of mine who live in Cortina, credible sources indicate that Leonardo da Vinci stopped here a few centuries ago—and that the pointy mountains in the background of the **Mona Lisa** are actually the Dolomites!

Although there's no real proof of this, it's enough to excite my imagination. I can almost see the entire panorama through da Vinci's eyes. What a spectacle!

## Discovering the Dolomites
The true fortune of these mountains arrived in 1956 with the Winter Olympics, when the residents of the area realized that tourism was going to play a huge role in their future. And so it has. The region is prosperous and well organized for visitors, with plenty of

*Rifugi offer shelter, warm hospitality, and delicious food.*

things to do and see. Great ski resorts are available in winter, and in summer you have your choice of easy to challenging hikes or climbs. Trails are well signed, and serious hikers can take advantage of a string of little Alpine houses called *rifugi*. These are cozy places where you can stop for a strudel and coffee (or a beer) before continuing your hike. Go to dolomiti.it/en/refuge to

find a listing of *rifugi* to visit or book for an overnight stay. If you're just planning a daytime stop, you don't need to book in advance.

To me, being in the Dolomites is like being Alice in Wonderland—extraordinary colors transforming from season to season, enchanting glaciers, imperial forests, emerald green lakes—and the best drinking water in the world! Adorable

*The Three Peaks of Lavaredo are truly magnificent.*

Tyrolean villages invite one to stop at one of their little cafés for steamy, creamy hot chocolate or delicious goulash, served by smiling and welcoming people. This is a great place to bring kids, too—they'll thank you forever!

Being in the Dolomites elevates one to a whole different level—not only in altitude, but truly in spirit. It makes you realize that you're so lucky to be in this world and able to see with your own eyes what amazing gifts God has given us. When you reach the highest points in the Dolomites, you feel as if you're literally reaching up and touching the face of God! If you have the chance to visit a delightful area called *Tre Cime de Lavaredo* (Three Peaks of Lavaredo), you'll enjoy the best views in all the mountains. Situated above 7,500 feet, this area is accessible only from May through October.

There are several routes to the peaks from nearby villages, but the usual way to get there is from Monte Paterno over the Patern Pass.

My favorite time of the year to visit the Dolomites is around Christmas. You can organize your own spectacular visit during the holidays, or anytime, by going to visitdolomites.com/en and researching the many options for a trip to the Dolomites. For skiers, the Dolomiti Superski pass gives access to more than 750 miles of ski slopes and 450 ski lifts; for details, visit dolomitisuperski.com/en.

## A Taste of the Dolomites

When it comes to the pleasures of life, of course I have to suggest some foods for you to try when you visit the Dolomites. One local specialty is *Tris de Canederli*, three dumpling-style bread balls filled with speck, a special cured, smoked ham produced in South Tyrol. Usually these are served in broth. And if you're an adventurous eater, you'll want to sample a Dolomites trio of game meat—roasted deer (*cervo*), mountain goat (*stambecco* or *ibex*), and goat antelope (*chamois*).

You'll definitely want to have the *polenta*—"the bread of the Dolomites." You can enjoy this dish made from yellow cornmeal at any time of the year, but I especially love it in winter, grilled and sprinkled with Parmesan cheese or served with a tasty meat stew.

*Rifugio Averau is a delightful bed and breakfast in the heart of the Alps.*

*Cortina d'Ampezzo is a beautiful town nestled in gorgeous Alpine scenery.*

Dessert? Apple strudel is the delicious local specialty.

Rifugio Averau in the lovely Alpine province of Belluno is a place where you should not only eat the homemade pasta, but actually spend the night. Truly charming!

**RIFUGIO AVERAU**
*Via Enrico Mattei 26*
*32040 Borca di Cadore]*
**Website:** *www.dolomiti.org/*
*dengl/Cortina/laga5Torri/*
*ospitalita/Averau/*
**Phone:** *+39 0436 4660*
**Email:** *rifugio.averau@*
*dolomiti.org*

## Cortina d'Ampezzo

Let's explore one of my favorite childhood places. Cortina d'Ampezzo is right in the heart of the Dolomites. This beautiful mountain resort, famous for its panoramic views and magnificent ski trails, was host to the 1956 Winter Olympics and has been the setting for some classic movies. The elegant village is a favorite vacation spot for

European aristocratic families, and its shops represent some of the most prestigious names in fashion, such as Gucci and Benetton. The artisan and craft shops and antique stores here are fun to explore.

To add a little historic background, during the Middle Ages the region of Ampezzo fell under the jurisdiction of the Holy Roman Empire. In 1420 the village was taken over by the Republic of Venice, and then in 1508 it was conquered by Austria, remaining in its control until 1920. Ampezzo never became a German-speaking territory but preserved its original language, Ladin. You feel a strong sense of history as you walk through Cortina,

## A Perfect Day in Cortina (the Best of the Dolomites!)

» You can start the day, by hopping on the main cable car, the Faloria, up to the ski lodge. The lodge is perched on a ridge at 2123 meters (6,965 feet)—at this elevation you truly feel like you're on top of the world and the view is beyond description!

» Enjoy a fantastic meal at Da Aurelio restaurant, located at 2175 meters (7,135 feet), with even higher peaks beyond. Da Aurelia is a family-owned chalet offering great food. You can even spend the night and explore nearby amazing trails!

*Despite its charmingly quaint appearance, Cortina is frequented by aristocratic visitors and offers some of the most sophisticated shopping in Europe.*

## ON LOCATION THE DOLOMITES

MOVIE *For Your Eyes Only*
RELEASE **1981**
DIRECTOR **John Glen**
CAST: **Roger Moore, Carole Bouquet, Topol, Julian Glover**

Bond, his name is James Bond—in Italy! We Italians feel quite proud that our country has hosted quite a few exciting scenes in the iconic James Bond franchise, this time starring the charming Roger Moore. *For Your Eyes Only* includes action sequences involving various winter sports. In a famous chase sequence, Bond (Moore)—on skis—is pursued by assassins riding spike-wheeled motorcycles. And the town of Cortina d'Ampezzo was the scene of the first attack on Bond and his partner Melina (Carole Bouquet).

Of course, the title theme song "For Your Eyes Only," sung by Sheena Easton is a must-have.

*The winter scenes in the movie were actually shot during the summer, so the producers had to rent large trucks to collect snow from the mountains and then dump it onto the streets of Cortina.*

*The ski jump and bobsled run in the movie are nowhere near each other in Cortina, despite appearances in the film.*

*In the movie, Bond and Melina are chased by cars in the mountains near Madrid, in Spain. Yet when one of the pursuing cars hurtles down a cliff and into a net where olives are being harvested, the farmers can clearly be heard swearing and talking in Italian, not Spanish!*

both in visible remnants from the Roman Empire and in the traditions and heritage held close by the local people.

## One Special Holiday

When I was a teenager, my mother decided to surprise me by booking a special Christmas concert in a lovely theater in San Candido, very close to Cortina D'Ampezzo.

I was so excited to arrive in this fairytale location, surrounded by frozen crystal lakes and lit by oil lamps at night! I remember my state of wonder when I looked out my window around 10 o'clock at night and saw hundreds of lanterns being carried by skiers. All those pretty lights illuminated the white snow in a wonderful framework of mountains, pine trees, and charming little chalets.

I recall the extremely warm hospitality of the Tyrolean owners of the chalet where

*A pub sign in Ladin, the ancient native Romance dialect of Cortina. Roughly translated, it says "A good inn and good companions are what everyone looks for, old and young."*

I stayed with my mother. I marveled upon entering my bedroom, with its white and cream-colored pillows and sheets—made of the softest flannel I've ever felt on my skin. There was a robe of softest wool to wear as I sat before the large fireplace and breathed in the sweet smells of hot chocolate and apple strudel, putting me completely into the holiday spirit. Every night at dinnertime, a large Austrian-German woman wearing a traditional Tyrolese dress served us Austrian sausages, goulash, and potatoes. She also served hot cider—but I doubt that that was what she was drinking. I noticed that her nose was truly red, most probably because of the heavy grappa she'd drunk to keep warm!

### Did You Know?

- Ernest Hemingway began writing his short story "Out of Season" in Cortina d'Ampezzo.

- Audrey Hepburn was a frequent visitor to Cortina.

*Bolzano is the largest city in the Alta Adige/South Tyrol region.*

*The Olympic Ice Stadium, where James Bond met villain Aris Kristatos in For Your Eyes Only.*

*Construction of the Gothic cathedral in Bolzano began in 1184 and was completed in the early 1500s.*

The truth of the matter is that the hospitality you receive here at any *rifugio*, resort, or chalet is going to conquer your heart. And when you wake up in the morning and look out your window, the picture you see will become a lasting memory.

## Bolzano

Not far to the west is the city of Bolzano, famous for Ötzi the iceman—a real man chipped out of a glacier in 1991 after being buried in the ice for more than 5,000 years! It is truly amazing to see this mummified statue, kept inside a frozen cell to preserve its fresh "old" look. Go to iceman.it to learn more about the incredible discovery. You can visit Ötzi at the South Tyrol Museum of Archeology in Bolzano, Tuesday–Sunday from 10 am to 6 pm (daily in July, August, and December).

## South Tyrol Museum of Archaeology

*Via Museo 43*
*39100 Bolzano*
**Website:**
   *archaeologiemuseum.it*
**Phone:** *+39 0471 320100*
**Email:** *info@iceman.it*

For more things to do in Bolzano, check out the tripadvisor.com website and type in "South Tyrol" in the search box. You'll be presented with several enticing options.

## Getting to the Dolomites

Cortina is the main travel center of the Dolomites, and from here it's easy to get to the region's other attractions. From

## That Colorful Feline...

Not only is Cortina d'Ampezzo where James Bond found his love, but this scenic town was also one of the stars in 1963's *The Pink Panther*. The Miramonti Hotel in Cortina was among the locations used in the movie, which was directed by Blake Edwards and featured David Niven, Peter Sellers, Robert Wagner, Capucine, and Claudia Cardinale. The original *Pink Panther* movie went on to spawn a long-running successful film franchise, turning Peter Sellers into an international star.

*Hotel Miramonti in Cortina, featured in both* For Your Eyes Only *and* The Pink Panther.

In this most romantic of settings, you can be warmed by white flannel sheets in elegant bedrooms at welcoming chalets and mountain hotels. The food is delicious. If you find yourself in one of the smaller, family-owned bed and breakfast inns, you'll likely be fed Austrian goulash, sausages, and *Kartoffeln* (German for potatoes). The hotels listed here are all close to one another, but you'll need a car to get from place to place.

If you really want to enjoy the Dolomites in style and luxury, you'll love these two five-star hotels. The food at both is out of this world!

### HOTEL & SPA ROSA ALPINA

This hotel in San Cassiano village has been owned by the Pizzinini family for three generations. Daily rates: €285–€1,200 including breakfast.
*Strada Micura de Rü 20
39030 San Cassiano
(Alto Adige)*
**Website:** *rosalpina.it*
**Phone:** + 39 0471 849500
**Email:** *alpina@
relaischateaux.com*

### CASTEL FRAGSBURG

This 17th-century hunting lodge transformed into a 20-room hotel has been owned by the Ortner family since 1955. Daily rates: €165–€300 including breakfast and dinner.
*Via Fragsburg 3
39012 Merano (Alto Adige)*
**Website:** *fragsburg.com*
**Phone:** +390473 244071
**Email:** *info@fragsburg.com*

## Romina's Hotel Picks

### Bolzano

If you'd like to spend a couple of days in the seductive Bolzano area, check out these two hotel options located close to the archaeology museum:

### PARKHOTEL LAURIN

*Via Laurin 4
39100 Bolzano*
**Website:** *laurin.it/en*
**Phone:** +39 0471 311000
**Email:** *info@laurin.it*

### HOTEL MONTE PARACCIA

*Via al Plan Dessora 41
Marebbe
39030 Bolzano*
**Website:** *paraccia.com*
**Phone:** +39 0474 501018
**Email:** *info@paraccia.com*

Milan, Cortina is best reached by taking the train to Venice, a 2 1/2-hour trip. (Purchase tickets and investigate itineraries online at trenitalia.com.) Then catch the "Cortina Express" direct bus from the Venice train station (Venezia Mestre), a 2 1/4-hour ride. (For schedule and fare information, visit cortinaexpress.it.)

You can also take the train all the way from Milan to Dobbiaco (called Toblach, in German)—6 hours, with two train changes. (I don't really recommend this if you aren't familiar with the area.) Then take local bus No. 445 to Cortina, a 50-minute ride.

## The Bond Palate

Champagne and oysters are among the things enjoyed by Bond and his love interest in *For Your Eyes Only*, so here's a delicious oyster recipe to cook for family and friends after you return home from your Italian holiday. To stick with all things Italian, look for the best Italian spumante in the market; Asti Cinzano, the most delicious Italian sparkling wine, is perfect for dessert!

### Oyster Stew

#### Ingredients

3 large potatoes, diced

2 pints of oysters, immersed in dry sherry (or any other liqueur you prefer)

2 cloves of minced garlic

½ cup of chopped parsley

4 cups of chicken broth or vegetable stock

4 teaspoons of slightly salted butter

½ cup of buttermilk

A quart of whole milk

A quart of cream

Salt and pepper, as per your preference

#### Preparation

After soaking for 20 minutes, remove the oysters from the liqueur.

On a pan, melt the butter, and add the salt and pepper onto the oysters. Sauté them in the butter until they curl up a bit.

Remove the oysters from the stove. Do not throw away the juice and liqueur from the oysters; they are needed later in the recipe.

Cook the potatoes until soft.

While the potatoes are still hot, move them into a larger pot. Add to this the buttermilk, butter, garlic, and broth, plus any additional seasonings you enjoy.

Once all the ingredients are together, mash them as if you were going to make mashed potatoes.

Add the cream to the pot and whisk it all on a low heat, until you obtain a dense mixture. At this point you add the cooked oysters in, the juice and liqueur from the oysters, and the whole milk.

Keep stirring until the soup becomes like a stew.

Season as you please. *Buon Appetito!*

# 7

# Rome, the mother of Italy . . . and backdrop for the greatest movies

*"All roads lead to Rome."* —Proverb

## ROME

Rome is the mother of all cities, in my opinion. Every year millions of people come from all around the world to see its monuments—incredible testaments to ancient human history—and to experience its culture. You'll find that Roman people are open, friendly, and very direct! They are extremely proud of their city and the beauty it possesses.

Rome is covered in history, with monuments, museums,

### · · · MOVIES · · · · · · · · · · · ·

Roman Holiday
La Dolce Vita
Once Upon a Time in America
Three Coins in the Fountain
When in Rome
To Rome with Love
Eat Pray Love
Pope John XXIII

## ON LOCATION ROME

MOVIE: *Roman Holiday*
RELEASE: **1953**
DIRECTOR: **William Wyler**
CAST: **Audrey Hepburn, Gregory Peck, Eddie Albert**

Who doesn't remember the adorable and elegant Audrey Hepburn and the sexy and attractive Gregory Peck in this sweet adventure story filmed entirely in Rome? The action revolves around a sort of impossible love between a young woman who is soon to become a queen and American reporter Joe Bradley (Gregory). Princess Anne (Audrey) is unhappy because because her royal duty will keep her from being able to enjoy a life of freedom. Bradley initially hopes to score a big scoop by breaking an exclusive story about the princess, with the help of his photographer friend Irving (Eddie Albert). But it's inevitable that they fall in love! You will sense the spirit of this story as soon as you step into Rome.

*Audrey Hepburn won the Academy Award as best actress for her portrayal of Princess Anne. The film won three Oscars and was nominated for ten.*

*This movie ranks #4 on the American Film Institute's Top 100 Love Stories. Audrey Hepburn is third on AFI's 50 Greatest Screen Legends (female). Gregory Peck ranks twelfth for male Legends*

*A day in Rome should make you smile as wide as Audrey Hepburn!*

and churches surrounding you wherever you go. You'll find yourself wanting to take a picture practically every time you turn around—so it's no wonder that so many directors have chosen to film their movies in this fantastic city.

## Roman Holiday on Foot

In an elegant and fluid way, *Roman Holiday* shows the many faces of Rome. Get ready to do some serious walking for your tour of this movie's locations—and be sure to wear comfortable shoes. The incredible scenery will help you forget about your sore feet; after all, it's Rome!

One of the best things you can do to discover all the pleasures of Rome is to make your base a hotel in the center of the city. One of my favorite Roman hotels is **Hotel Sonya**, with has great service and hospitality, excellent food, and is very, very comfortable. Even if you decide not to stay there, Hotel Sonya's strategic location is a great starting point to see the entire city.

Not only is this hotel located in the very heart of Rome, it's placed in the safest area of the city, just a short walk away from Termini train station, and walking distance from the magnificent **Trevi Fountain**, the Colosseum, Spanish Steps, Piazza Venezia, and all other major sights in Rome. You can see it all by walking from Hotel Sonya, saving quite a bit on bus fare and public transportation.

But if you're going to do a lot of walking in Rome, keep your comfort in mind. In the summertime, temperatures in Rome range from 77 degrees Fahrenheit all the way into the 90s! And it doesn't cool off in the nighttime. So wear the right

## ON LOCATION ROME

MOVIE: *Three Coins in the Fountain*
RELEASE: 1954
DIRECTOR: Jean Negulesco
CAST: Clifton Webb, Jean Peters

This is definitely one of my favorite movies. The movie, starring Clifton Webb and Jean Peters, narrates the stories of three American girls, working in Rome and dreaming of finding their eternal love in the eternal city!

In *Three Coins in the Fountain*, the three women stop by the famous **Trevi Fountain**, and each of them throws a coin into the fountain, wishing to find love. This memorable scene has inspired millions of tourists to come back to Rome—some *each* year—and toss in a coin (I guess that fountain now should be more money than water!).

Now for some fun bits of trivia about this movie:

Additional locations for *Three Coins in the Fountain* include the Dolomites, Bolzano, and Venice. You'll learn a lot about these amazing places in this book. The inside scenes were all filmed in Cinecittà Studios in the heart of Rome, where all the movie studios are located and most of the films are shot.

Did you know that the great Frank Sinatra recorded the theme song for this movie and did not get credited for it? I really love this song, and re-recorded it for my Italy album.

*Three Coins in the Fountain* won three Academy Awards: Best Song, Best Picture, and Best Cinematography.

Italian handsome Rossano Brazzi was also one of the stars of this movie. He appeared in many wonderful pictures during that time.

There was a delicious appetizer created in one of the scenes—a baked concoction of shrimp, langostinos, artichoke hearts, mushrooms, and spinach in a cream-sherry sauce. So delicious!

*Three Coins in the Fountain* also inspired the 2010 film, *When in Rome*, which tells the story of a woman who reverses the process and, instead of throwing the coins into a fountain, picks them up from a fountain of love (built only for this movie) in Rome. Naturally, through this reversed process she gets a man she doesn't want! That film starred Josh Duhamel and Kristen Bell.

*A dramatic night view of the magnificent Trevi Fountain.*

cific things you want to do that day of the trip and prepared in advance, (e.g., shopping, museums, restaurants, etc). Remember to keep everything under control and your wallet in front and not in your back pocket!

Another idea mentioned earlier but worth repeating is to carry a copy of your passport instead of the original. Losing your passport is a huge headache. It's also a good idea to leave copies of your passport and other important documents with a friend at home, so, if needed, your friend can fax your documents to you. And to be on the safe side, always carry with you the phone number of the American consulate in Rome.

If you plan to spend at least one week in Rome, you'll need around $350 to cover lunches, dinners, snacks, admission to museums and other sites, and public transportation—and that's a conservative estimate,

kind of clothes for hot weather. For men, lightweight shirts and trousers would do the trick, and don't forget the trendy sunglasses! Women should go for light cotton sundresses. Do not wear jeans, during summertime especially, because of the humidity—you will find them very uncomfortable. Also avoid wearing black clothing as they will attract the sun and you will sweat like crazy! A lightweight cotton tunic or looser clothes will be cooler and much more comfortable. Bring hats to protect your head from the heat.

In winter, a couple of sweaters, warm scarves, and warm hats would do very well for you.

As you plan your walking tour of Rome, remember that cobblestones are pretty much everywhere so wear comfortable, low-heeled shoes. Do not bring many credit cards with you, and the cash you bring should be allocated to the spe-

**TRAVEL TIP** My advice for the ladies: don't wear heels when walking in Rome (unless you've been invited to a gala event). Pretty much all the streets are made of cobblestones, so they are very difficult to walk on if you are wearing fashionable high heels. Make smart choices and be comfortable.

*The Spanish Steps are one of the best-known landmarks of Rome.*

*This view from the top of the Spanish Steps shows the Fontana della Barcaccia, and the narrow street in the distance is the shopper's paradise of the Via dei Condotti.*

here to eat! These restaurants are notoriously created just for tourists, with incredibly overpriced menus—and the food is not really very good.

There are many hotels in Rome (see pages 65–66), but if you want to be close to the most incredible attractions in the atmosphere of this romantic movie, you might want to stay at the **Hotel Romanico Palace** right across Piazza Venezia at the center of the city (Via Boncompagni 37, hotelromanico.com; around $150 per night). Or you could find a cute hotel near the metro station.

The metro will take you right into the heart of the area. As you face the steps, you'll see **Via Margutta**, the little street where Joe Bradley (Gregory Peck) lived in a small apartment at Number 51. (Today the street is occupied by many street artists, psychics,

assuming that you're really careful with your money. A trip to via dei Condotti will get you an inch of a glove for that amount, so watch where your money is going.

But if you don't mind spending money, then… abracadabra! Don't let me hold you back from crazy spending. Even I fall for that. Go ahead and have the time of your life—you only live once, right?

Our first location is the **Spanish Steps**, 135 broad steps ascending from the Piazza di Spagna to the church of Trinita dei Monti. This is the scene in *Roman Holiday* where you see Gregory and Audrey (ice cream cone in hand) come down a very long set of steps. From here, you can look out on the whole city. It is truly a magnificent place to be.

Once you go all the way down the steps—which will give you a great workout, by the way—you will find a few cute little restaurants. Don't stop

*A rare view of the charming Via Margutta covered in snow.*

and little shops.) You could be lucky enough to find the gate open so you can visit the courtyard and perhaps even to go up the stairs and to the terrace of the apartment where Princess Anne and Joe Bradley shared a night together. ("I've never been alone with a man before, even with my dress on. With my dress off, it's most unusual," stated the Princess.) Caution: This is actually a private residence, so if you do enter the courtyard, you'll have to sneak in. This is a secret, so don't tell anyone I told you.

It's not far from here to **Via dei Condotti**, known as the

*The Pantheon. A Latin inscription reads "Marcus Agrippa, son of Lucius, built this when consul for the third time."*

most expensive part of the city, the "Beverly Hills of Rome." All the greatest designers and brands are represented on Via Condoitti, from Valentino to Armani, Rolex to Dolce & Gabbana. Perhaps you'll be persuaded to spend everything you have on that amazing Gucci purse!

Soon you will come to what I think is the most breathtaking fountain ever sculpted—the **Trevi Fountain**, known for the old superstition that if you throw a coin into its water, you will return to Rome and make your dreams come true. In *Roman Holiday*, Princess Anne

has her hair cut right across from the fountain. What an unforgettable scene! By the way, that barbershop is still there. And you can definitely throw your own coins into the fountain—but be careful what you wish for.

Gelato time! You can find what is arguably the best gelato in Rome at **San Crispino Gelato** (Via della Panetteria 42, phone 066-793-924), a couple streets to the right of the Trevi heading toward the Quirinale Palace. This ice cream parlor is so small that is is very easy to miss it, and this is not a place you want to miss. Once

you are there, you will definitely become like a baby in a candy store. The honey flavor is to die for! When you taste this ice cream, a sudden sense of exquisiteness overwhelms you—it grabs you and begs for more. Even when you feel that your jeans are tight and that you had enough ice cream for the next three years, you can't help yourself! You'll know what Julia Roberts felt after stopping here with her ice cream in *Eat, Pray, Love!* (see page 70). It's paradise all around you, with pistachio, licorice, honey, and tiramisu ice cream. Yes, it's a tsunami of flavors, an invasion of your palate, as chocolate praline and sugary chocolate almonds melt in your mouth, while a delicious caramel fills your senses. There are no survivors. You fall victim to its goodness, and you tell yourself that tomorrow is another day and the you'll start the diet. For me, that unfortunately

---

### La Dolce Trevi

You might recall a sexy scene in the magnificent 1960 film *La Dolce Vita*, directed by the late genius Federico Fellini. Beautiful actress Anita Ekberg enters the water of the Trevi Fountain at night, leaving costar Marcello Mastroianni completely shocked. That is definitely a movie to watch, and it will take you to many of the same areas you see in *Roman Holiday*. But please, don't enter the fountain at night, or you'll be arrested!

never worked! Did I tempt your senses enough now? You *must* go and have an ice cream at San Crispino Gelato.

Now we continue south to the **Pantheon**, built as a temple to the Roman gods nearly 2000 years ago. The well-preserved structure with its massive dome has been used as a Catholic church since the seventh century. The café from *Roman Holiday* where the two stars shot a few scenes—including Peck's line, "Champagne per la signorina, and cold coffee for me"—is no longer here, but you'll find some really delicious eating places in the area. Two famed coffee bars are close at hand. **Caffe Sant'Eustachio** (Piazza Sant'Eustachio 82)—featured in *Eat Pray Love*—is known for its grand caffe and grand cappuccino, made according to a highly guarded recipe.

**Tazza d'Oro** (Via degli Orfani 84), often said to serve Rome's best espresso, is famous for its coffee granita. A great gelateria is nearby: **Gelateria della Palma** (Via della Maddalena 20) has at least 100 flavors of gelato and semifreddo.

If you feel like taking a break to spend some time in a shopping mall, there's the **Euroma2**, with about 230 shops (mainly clothes and accessories) and restaurants, located near the EUR district. If you start from the Pantheon, it's a half-hour walk to the Termini rail station. Take the Metro B line from Termini to the EUR Palasport station, cross the road, and board one of the frequent free buses to the mall (a 5 to 15-minute ride). In addition to the shopping and food, the mall's air conditioning and free toilets can be a welcome relief.

Back on your walking tour, the Lungotevere road stretches along the right bank of the Tiber River, and at **Ponte Sant'Angelo** you'll see the great round fortress of **Castel Sant'Angelo** across the river. Completed in 139 AD as a mausoleum for Emperor Hadrian, this structure served as the backdrop for Princess Anne's evening of music and dancing on a river barge. (Word to the wise: don't descend too far down the steps to the river if you don't like unpleasant odors!)

The next stop is the **Mouth of Truth** in Trastevere (by the way, did you know that Academy Award winning legendary film composer Ennio Morricone, with whom

 **TRAVEL TIP** How many books have their own soundtrack? Well, this one does (in a manner of speaking)! My album from Lakeshore Records, *Where Did They Film That? Italy— The Music Journey*, boasts my versions all of the most famous theme songs from the movies described in this book: *Romeo and Juliet, Cinema Paradiso, Il Postino, Three Coins in the Fountain,* and many others. Now as you explore your way through Italy with this book, and visit the marvelous sights and incredible movie locations, you can also hear the songs of the movies in your iPod or mp3 player!

*The Castel Sant'Angelo, as seen from the Ponte Sant'Angelo.*

In the Roman Forum, you can walk in the footsteps of Caesar, Cicero, and many great Romans of ancient times.

else! And be sure to take plenty of pictures.

The **Roman Forum** was the original meeting place of Joe Bradley and Princess Anne, where she lay on the stone quoting poetry, seemingly drunk. If you've not visited this historic sight already, you may want to return another day so you can devote more time to it, along with the **Colosseum**. (For a romantic view, return in the evening to enjoy the vista from Capitoline Hill.) Joe Bradley brought Princess Anne to the Colosseum during their day-long holiday. The colossal monument has been the backdrop for so many famous movies and TV specials that it is surely the best-known symbol of Italy around the world. Take in its immensity and ponder its sheer presence after 2,000 years.

Continue walking on the north side, past Trajan's Market and the luminous white

I had the honor and pleasure to make an entire record, was born in Trastevere?). The legend is that if you're given to lying, when you put your hand in the open mouth of this ancient stone face it will be bitten off. Since childhood, this particular piece of history has enchanted me, the thought that if someone had lied to me they would eventually lose a hand in the Mouth of Truth! In *Roman Holiday*, the statue

is a challenge for our two stars, neither of whom is being truthful to the other.

This popular attraction is located in the portico of the sixth-century church of Santa Maria in Cosmedin, in the Piazza Bocca della Verita. And remember, when you stick your hand inside, tell the truth—or

The Mouth of Truth, as it looks today...

... and as seen in Roman Holiday, with Gregory Peck horrifying Audrey Hepburn.

memorial to Vittorio Emanuele, to the **Palazzo Colonna** at the foot of Quirinal Hill (in Piazza SS Apostoli). This palace was used for the unforgettable interior scenes at the end of *Roman Holiday*, when Princess Anne holds a press conference and discovers the true identities of Joe and Irving. To see it, you must arrive on Saturday morning, as it is now a museum that is open only from 9 am to 1 pm on that one day. If you're a late sleeper, well, too bad!

## The Vatican

Although it's not mentioned in *Roman Holiday*, the Vatican is without a doubt something that will take your breath away. Of course, you know that **Vatican City** is a tiny independent state on the west side of the Tiber. Just like any other state, it has its own bank, pharmacy, and post office within its tall walls. The Vatican's palaces were originally built for Renaissance popes starting with Julius

*The Palazzo Colonna, location of the final scene of* Roman Holiday *and home to a splendid art collection.*

II in the early 16th century; additions were made in the 18th century.

The Vatican Museums contain some of the world's most important art, from the Michelangelo ceiling frescoes in the **Sistine Chapel** to an astonishing collection of Renaissance paintings. **Saint Peter's Basilica**, one of the world's largest churches, houses Michelangelo's *Pieta*.

The Vatican is closed every Sunday except for a few times throughout the year. Before you make your plans, check the Vatican website for any tours and/or special events. The well-organized site offers

*The Colosseum, venue for centuries of gladiator battles, is one of the most impressive relics of the Roman Empire.*

**TRAVEL TIP** The ticket line for the Colosseum is *very* long. To avoid standing in it, go to the Palatine Hill ticket office (up the street from the Colosseum, past the Arch of Constantine) and buy a combo ticket for the Colosseum, Palatine Hill, and Roman Forum. You will save yourself hours because you can bypass the line if you already have your ticket in hand.

*St. Peter's Basilica, the holiest of Catholic churches and the heart of Vatican City.*

a great deal of information, including how to get there from anywhere you are staying in Rome; go to www.vatican.va.

Note that the Vatican Museums no longer accept credit or debit cards for tickets purchased at the site; you can use cash or, even better, buy your tickets in advance on the website.

The closest Metro stop to the museum entrance is Cipro-Musei Vaticani near Piazza Santa Maria delle Grazie. Bus 49 stops near the entrance and tram 19 also stops nearby. A number of buses go close to Vatican City.

The office for all Vatican City Tourist Information is on the left side of St. Peter's Square and has lots of great information and a small shop selling maps, guides, souvenirs, and jewelry. Tourist information is open Monday–Saturday, 8:30 am to 6:30 pm.

By the way, the **Vatican City Post Office is** the Speedy Gonzales of post offices compared with the rest of Italy, and a must for anyone who's into the stamps of different countries. There's a branch of the post office in the museum, or look for the yellow *Poste Vaticane* boxes in St. Peter's Square.

## Too Much Walking? Take the Bus

If the massive *Roman Holiday* tour that I've described involves more walking than you can possibly do, there's a way for you to rest a bit while getting to your destinations.

Begin at the Spanish Steps and take the metro from there to the Colosseom stop. View the Colosseum, the Forum, and the Mouth of Truth as noted. Buses 23, 64, and 280 all cruise both sides of the Tiber, so catch a bus up to Castel Sant'Angelo. To continue to the locations in the Centro district, you can pick up bus 116; this little blue bus wends its way through Centro with stops at the Piazza Navona area, the Trevi Fountain, and all the major historical sites.

**TRAVEL TIP** When you visit the Vatican church and museum, make sure that your knees and shoulders are covered or your entrance will be declined (true for both men and women). Go to www.vatican.va to learn about do's and don'ts that you should respect.

Michelangelo's Pieta, one of the greatest Renaissance sculptures.

The Creation of Adam, the most famous panel on the ceiling of the Sistine Chapel.

It's not impossible to meet Pope Francis, if you're willing to plan ahead.

## Meet the Pope

If you want the most exciting visit to the Vatican possible, you simply must pay a visit to His Holiness the Pope. The most revered personage in the Roman Catholic Church, a world historical figure, and a frequent visitor to presidents and kings, the Pope may seem in a completely different world to the ordinary traveler, but in fact it is perfectly possible to request an audience with His Holiness.

However, possible does not mean easy. Audiences with the Pope are available only on Wednesday mornings, and tickets have to be reserved way ahead of time—you can imagine how many people want an opportunity to meet the Pope.

You can arrange an audience with the Pope through the **Prefecture of the Pontifical House of the Vatican City**: Tel: 39-06-698-83017. Or you can visit www.vatican.va and fill out a web form.

### Did You Know?

Rome was built on seven ancient hills: Quirinal (location of the Presidential palace and other government buildings), Palatine, Esquiline, Aventine, Caelian, Viminal, and Capitoline. Famed tenor Mario Lanza starred in a 1957 movie called *Seven Hills of Rome*.

## ON LOCATION ROME

In April 2002, another movie was filmed in Rome (yes, over 135 American movies so far have been filmed in Rome), this one a TV movie titled *Pope John XXIII ( Papa Giovanni)*. This movie narrates the story of a deeply spiritual man and priest who rose from poverty to become the Pope for the Roman Catholic Church!

The man who played John Paul XXIII is a fantastic and brilliant actor who I have the pleasure and honor to know, a man who also has a unique sense of humor—the one and only Ed Asner.

### INTERVIEW WITH ED ASNER

1. As we all well know, you had the wonderful opportunity to play Pope John XXIII with acclaimed success. How hard was it to transition from being yourself to being your incredible character?
   **EA: The demands were minimal so I just conjured up my own holiness and let it run amok. Constraint was the clue.**

2. Since this movie was filmed in Italy, what do you recall about your experience there, and is there any place you particularly loved or enjoyed while working there?
   **EA: Italy was a beautiful arena to work in, and since I was surrounded by the holiness and the beauty, all I really had to do was show I was breathing.**

3. Would you go back to Italy on vacation? If so, where would you like to visit?
   **EA: I no longer like to travel, but I would go back to Italy. And I have a friend in Breda Di Piave.**

*Pope John XXIII* was partly filmed in the breathtaking **Palazzo Farnese**, in Rome. Since 1939, the Palazzo has been used by the French as their embassy. This building is considered the most spectacular example of High Renaissance architecture in Italy.

Designed and built in 1517 for the Farnese family, this incredible building has been adorned with work by the most honorable architects of all time, including the one and only Michelangelo. Alessandro Farnese, the owner, was appointed cardinal in 1493, when he was only 25 years old. He came from an extremely wealthy family and lived just like a prince—until the famous Sack of Rome took everything he has ever had.

A little trivia about this historical palazzo?

Did you know that the famous opera by Puccini, *Tosca* (1900), especially the confrontation between the heroine of the opera and the malevolent chief of police, Scarpia, takes place in Palazzo Farnese?

As mentioned, the Palazzo is home to the French embassy, under terms of a 99-year agreement lease. The French government pays the Italian government a symbolic fee of 1 euro per month!

Be aware that most of the guided tours to this beautiful palazzo are delivered in French and Italian, and only a few are in English. It takes about 45 minutes to see the Palazzo, but you must book tickets far in advance. And be sure to find out if the galleries and the museum inside will be open. Sometimes only part of the palace is opened up, leaving out the very best to see. It costs 5 Euros to get in.

Piazza Farnese

67, 00100 Roma, Italy, +39 06 0606 0884

---

*While I am Italian, I never heard about the city of Breda Di Piave that Ed Asner mentioned above, so I went to explore the area a bit and I have to say that it is like a little piece of paradise. Located in the Venetian region, Breda is a strip of land with an abundance of water and springs. Artists have always characterized this land with brushstrokes of green and blue that, in the changing of the seasons, take on the colors of the Venetian countryside. It is truly a rich and beautiful part of Italy.*

*The Aurelian Walls were built around the Pyramid of Cestius, centuries after the pyramid was originally constructed.*

## Unknown Rome

One of the advantages of reading this book is that you're dealing with a true Italian girl who can take you straight to places you would never imagine existed in this beautiful city.

But I'm afraid I can't take you to an unbelievable event I witnessed in Rome in 2012. For the first time in twenty-six years, a snowstorm covered Rome in white. The Colosseum looked like something out of a fairy tale. Very magical!

Even if you don't see snow in Rome, here are some other "unknown" sights for you to discover.

The best time to visit the following attractions is usually in the warm but not too hot month of May or perhaps September.

**Pyramid of Cestius—** One of Rome's lesser-known attractions will blow your mind! Who says you need to go to Egypt (or as someone else might say, Vegas) to see a pyramid? Rome has the fantastic Pyramid of Cestius, completed around 12 BC as a tomb for a magistrate named Gaius Cestius. The 120-foot-high marble-cloaked pyramid is in the southern part of Rome next to the Aurelian Wall and Protestant Cemetery.

**Piazza Navona—**This site of a first-century Roman circus (oval competition arena) isn't too far from Trevi Fountain, the Colosseum, and the center of

## Guards! Guards!

One of the most picturesque traditions of Vatican City is the Pontifical Swiss Guard. These Swiss volunteers have guarded the Pope since 1506, and their formal uniforms of blue, red, and yellow doublet and breeches still have a Renaissance flair. Despite their medieval appearance, Swiss guards are actually highly trained modern security professionals. After the attempted assassination of Pope John Paul II in 1981, the Swiss Guards have placed much greater emphasis on the physical protection of the Pope, and they have received enhanced training in unarmed combat and small arms use.

Guard recruits must be practicing Roman Catholics, Swiss nationals, between 19 and 30 years of age, single, high school graduates, and at least 5 feet 8½ inches tall. Although I come from Italy, I have as much fun as any tourist taking pictures of these unique soldiers and their traditional uniforms. I don't think their regulations allow them to pose for pictures while they're on duty, but once in a while they make an exception to the rule!

*Despite his medieval uniform, this Swiss Guard is a trained modern security professional.*

the city. Even today, the piazza follows the stadium's original elliptical shape. Piazza Novona is best known for Bernini's majestic **Fountain of the Four Rivers**, unveiled in 1651. Four gods on the fountain's four corners represent the world's four major rivers, as known at the time.

If you saw the 2009 movie *Angels & Demons* starring Tom Hanks, you may remember that the obelisk atop the Four Rivers Fountain was the fourth Illuminati marker, and the fountain was where Cardinal Baggia was dumped in order to carry out his death by drowning.

*A detail of the base of the Fountain of the Four Rivers; the foremost figure represents the Ganges.*

Piazza Navona is the best place to refresh and relax during a crazy walking day in Rome. In fact, although still a magnificent place to visit for its ancient history, it's also one of the largest squares in Europe, and the space all around you lets your eyes rest and makes you feel calmer, as you can touch the fresh water of the fountain or drink from the side faucets of water attached to its walls. Pure and fresh water, a calm atmosphere for the eye and a place you can stare at for hours as its beauty will turn a cold statue with a static expression into the one of happiness and wonder. It is truly beautiful here.

**Museum of Purgatory—** Is there an afterlife? Let's try to be good people, you just never know. The tiny Museum of Purgatory is worth a visit if you're looking for something well off the beaten path. Taking

*The Chiesa del Sacro Cuore del Suffragio, home of the Museum of Purgatory.*

up just one wall of a small room in a church not far from the Vatican, the 100-year-old museum displays objects said to show contact from souls trapped between heaven and hell. A French priest, Victor Jouet, collected the relics throughout Europe; in 1912 he died in the room that holds them. • Chiesa del Sacro Cuore del Suffragio, Lungotevere Prati 12; usually open Monday–Friday, 7:30 to 11 am and 4 to 7 pm.

**Rome Criminal Museum—** In case you've been wondering how criminals have been dealt with over the centuries, you can find out at this museum operated by the Ministry of Justice in what was once a prison. Visit <u>museocriminologico.it</u> for details. • Via del Gonfalone 29; open Tuesday–Saturday from 9 am to 1 pm; also Tuesday and Thursday from 2:30 to 6:30 pm.

**TRAVEL TIP** You'll get thirsty with all the walking you'll be doing in Rome, so let me assure you that you can, without any hesitation, drink the water coming out of the little public wall fountains. Fountains are pretty much everywhere in Rome, and the water is delicious. The fountains look like your kitchen sink, and you can easily fill your water bottles from them. You don't have to spend extra euros for bottled water—Rome has the freshest and purest of water.

*The Fountain of the Turtles makes a cameo in* The Talented Mr. Ripley.

**Torre Argentina Cat Sanctuary—** Here's a cool spot for animal lovers to meet people who are making a difference in the lives of Rome's stray cats, and to take a tour of lesser-known Roman ruins at the same time. Volunteers from around the world help care for some 250 cats sheltered among ancient monuments (<u>romancats.com</u>). • Largo di Torre Argentina, corner of Via Florida and Via di Torre Argentina; visitors welcome daily from noon to 6 pm.

**Fountain of the Turtles—** In Piazza Mattei you can take a look at the most original fountain of all, the Fountain of the Turtles (Fontana della Tartarughe). According to popular legend, the graceful 16th-century fountain was built in a single night by order of Duke Muzio Mattei so that he could win the heart of a young lady who lived in the palace facing the square.

**Piazza del Popolo—** This is one of Rome's largest squares. The great Maestro Ennio Morricone has conducted his much-loved Roman Sinfonietta in concert here. You may also want to visit **Piazza Navona**, with its three beautiful fountains.

## Why Not Take to the Water?

If you plan to stay in Rome only for a day or two before proceeding to other beautiful parts of Italy and Europe, you can always hop on a Costa Cruises ship—the best of the best in large Italian cruise ships. Their elegance, entertainment, food, and itineraries are simply out of this world, and you will never find such a warm welcome anywhere else! I went on many of these cruises with my mother, and we enjoyed every second. Cruises depart from Civitavecchia port northwest of the city (<u>costacruise.com</u>).

## Rome's Best Eateries

You may have to extend your stay in Rome in order to try all these great restaurants!

- **Osteria del Gallo.** A haven just off the busy lanes west of Piazza Navona, the Osteria serves classy meals at a touch more than average tourist prices; Vicolo di Montevecchio, 27 (off Via di Tor Millina).
- **Dar Poeta.** Always busy but so good, a very simple place, not fancy, but with legendary pizzas and generous, filling bruschetta; Vicolo del Bologna (Trastevere).
- **Baffetto.** Some say Baffetto serves the best pizza in Rome, and often there are incredibly long lines; Via del Governo Vecchio.
- **Enoteca Antica.** A small wine bar–restaurant with a cozy atmosphere, Enoteca Antica serves good pizzas, reasonably priced, and gorgeous chocolate cake; Via della Croce (near the Spanish Steps).
- **Gusto.** This restaurant, pizzeria, wine bar, and bookshop has been around a few years now, but it's still a modish spot for Sunday brunch and also serves good dinners and pizzas. Outdoor tables are atmospherically located opposite the Mausoleum of Augustus; Piazza Augusta Imperatore 9, near Via del Corso.
- **Il Margutta**. Audrey Hepburn and Gregory Peck had dinner here. Expect to pay €120 for two, with wine; Via Margutta Roma 118.

- **Tanagra Caffè Concerto.** Enjoy opera being performed while you dine here. The food is delicious and the entertainment fantastic; Lungotevere Flaminio 57, tanagra.it.

Here are some additional places I recommend:

**Aristocampo** in Campo dei Fiori has the freshest and most delicious combinations of Italian panini (Via della Lungaretta, 75, Trastevere). In the San Lorento district, there's a phenomenal small pizza parlor called **Formula Uno** (Via degli Equi, 13). And if you love all kinds of delicious Italian salads,

**Insalata Rica** is a spectacle of salads in thousands of color and taste combinations. There are many locations throughout Rome. **Al Picchio** is one of the restaurants by Trevi Fountain that gives you the best food for your money (Via del Lavatore, 39/40; ristorantealpicchio.it).

## Rome for Food Lovers

For a unique Rome experience, sign up for an Italian cooking class or culinary tour. Several organizations in Rome (and some based in the U.S.) offer classes or food-oriented tours. The following two have full tour itineraries focused on food:

### Tipping Point

Strangely enough, when you dine out in Italy you don't leave a tip for your waiter. I know it sounds quite strange or rude, but waiters may take the tip as a form of disrespect. They are paid pretty well by the restaurants, so don't feel bad about not leaving extra money. If you really want to contribute, you can ask your server if you could leave him a little gift of money for the amazing job he did.

*Looking down on the Piazza del Popolo from the Pincian Hill.*

**TRAVEL TIP**

Romans love to shop, and you'll be absorbed by it, too, when you stroll along Via Nazionale. There are literally hundreds of stores lining this boulevard. But here's a little secret. At the open-air market in Via Cesare Balbo you can buy practically everything you want for a fraction of what you'd pay in the center of Rome on Via dei Condotti and Via del Corso .

By the way, be cautious about purchasing "Louis Vuitton" or "Gucci" bags on the streets of Rome. In Italy, buying fake copycat brands is not only illegal but is immediately punishable with high fines and even jail.

**ACTIVE GOURMET HOLIDAYS**
*One Gaidosz Way*
*Derby, CT 06418*
***Website:*** *activegourmet holidays.com*

**LE BACCANTI TOURS**
*Via Benedetto Naldini, 23*
*210 Rivington St. # 11*
*New York, NY 10002*
***Website:*** *lebaccanti.com*

Check the following websites for shorter culinary tours, cooking classes, workshops, and wine tastings:

- cookingclassesinrome.com (classes by Andrea Consoli, assisted by his American wife)
- contextrome.com (cuisine walks, wine tastings)

- maureenbfant.com (food tours, cooking classes)
- elizabethminchilliinrome.com (food tours, workshops)
- katieparla.com (food tours)
- vinoroma.com (food tours, wine tastings)

**TRAVEL TIP**

**Rome at Night**
If you like nightlife, you might want to check some areas that tourists don't really know about. **San Lorenzo** is the student area in Rome, where you will find an array of pubs and clubs. The historic **Trastevere** area is extremely trendy—in particular Piazza Santa Maria, with its famous Bar San Calisto.

## ON LOCATION ROME

MOVIE: *Once Upon a Time in America*
RELEASE: 1984
DIRECTOR: **Sergio Leone**
CAST: Elizabeth McGovern, Robert DeNiro, James Woods

It is my honor to pay respect to another incredibly talented director who is no longer with us but who gave us so much with his unbelievable vision and unstoppable energy. I am talking about Sergio Leone.

Sergio was born on January 3, 1929, in Tortella Dei Lombardi, in the Irpinia territory in Avellino province (near Naples)—and guess what? He went to school with my mentor, Academy Award–winning film composer Ennio Morricone. Sergio is the father of the popular "Spaghetti Western" movies, including *The Good, the Bad and the Ugly*, *For a Fistful of Dollars*, and *Once Upon a Time in the West*. Of course, the brilliant Maestro Morricone composed unforgettable music for all these movies—and honored me by asking me to write lyrics for some of the scores.

To my great surprise, I found out that almost all of these motion pictures were filmed in Spain. But the great director's last production, *Once Upon a Time in America*—despite the "America" in the title—was shot almost entirely in Italy, mostly in Rome. (Additional scenes were shot in Venice, Florida, and New York.) Once again, Morricone composed the music, and recently I was asked to write some lyrics. You can hear my salute to Sergio and my work with Maestro Morricone on my album *Morricone Uncovered*. The album includes, among others, the song "Ti Ho Amato" (which I wrote) from *Once Upon a Time in America*, as well as "Il Tempo Sa" from *A Fistful of Dollars*. Visit www. WhereDidTheyFilmThatItaly.com for more details!

The following are the best of the best when it comes to places to stay in Rome. They are all five-stars hotels, with service and elegance that will sweep you off your feet! Depending on season, from April through September, rates at these hotels can range from €350–€800 per night.

## ST. GEORGE ROMA

A harmonious mix of modernism and classicism. According to some sources, this is where Audrey Hepburn and Gregory Peck stayed while making *Roman Holiday*.
*Via Giulia 62*
*00186 Rome*
*Website: stgeorge.*
   *hotelinroma.com*

## JUMEIRAH GRAND HOTEL VIA VENETO

Classic luxury.
*Via Vittorio Veneto 155*
*00187 Rome*
*Website: jumeirah.com*

## GRAND HOTEL DE LA MINERVE

A 17th-century building near Piazza Navona, with rooftop terrace.
*Piazza Della Minerva 69*
*00186 Rome*
*Website: grandhoteldela*
   *minerve.com*

## HOTEL ALEPH

*Via di San Basilio 15*
*00100 Roma*
**Tel.** *+39 06 422 901*
**Fax** *+39 06 422 900 00*
**Email:** *reservation@aleph.*
   *boscolo.com*
**Website:** *www.*
   *boscolohotels.com*

## HOTEL D'INGHILTERRA

*Via Bocca di Leone, 14*
*00187 Rome*
**Tel.** *+39 06 699811*
**Fax** *+39 06 69922243*
**Email:** *reservation.hir@*
   *royaldemeure.com*
**Website:** *www.*
   *royaldemeure.com*

## HOTEL DE RUSSIE

*Via del Babuino, 9*
*00187 Rome*
**Tel.** *+39 06 328881*
**Fax** *+39 06 32888888*
**Email:** *reservations.*
   *derussie@roccoforte*
   *collection.com*
**Website:** *www.*
   *roccofortehotels.com*

## HOTEL EDEN

*Via Ludovisi, 49*
*00187 Rome*
**Tel.** *+39 06 478121*
**Fax** *+39 06 4821584*
**Email:** *1872.reservations@*
   *lemeridien.com*
**Website:** *www.hotel-eden.it*

 **Romina's Hotel Picks**

## HOTEL EXEDRA

*Piazza della Repubblica, 47*
*00100 Rome*
**Tel.** *+39 06 489 381*
**Fax** *+39 06 489 380 00*
**Email:** *reservation@*
   *exedra.boscolo.com*
**Website:** *www.*
   *boscolohotels.com*

## HOTEL PALAZZO MANFREDI

Guest or gladiator? This is a truly spectacular hotel.
- Luxury and romance in the heart of Rome
- The combination of classic Italian and contemporary design
- The suites and restaurant with view of the Colosseum
*Via Labicana 125*
*00184 Rome*
**Tel.** *+39 06 77591380*
**Fax** *+39 06 7005638*
**Email:** *info@*
   *hotelgladiatori.it*
**Website:** *www.*
   *hotelgladiatori.it*

---

**TRAVEL TIP** The Rome Tourism website has a link especially for kids. You might find something useful, too! Check it out (and lots more) at www.turismoroma.it.

These above are all the very best pick for me. They are all five stars hotels—you can't find any better. Their services and elegance just took over me!

The following hotels are less expensive than those listed above—about €130–€170 per night—but they still offer great service!

**ASA HOWARD HOTEL**
doubles (with shared bathrooms) from €170 room only
*Via Sistina 149,*
*Via Capo le Case 18*
*+39 06 699 24555*
*Website: casahoward.com*

**RELAIS PALAZZO TAVERNA HOTEL**
doubles from €100 room only
*Via dei Gabrielli 92*
*+39 06 203 98064*
*Website: relaispalazzo*
*taverna.com*

**BED & BREAKFAST HOTEL SANTA MARIA**
doubles from €100 B&B
*Vicolo del Piede 2*
*+39 06 589 4626*
*Website: www.*
*otelsantamariatrastevere.it*

**THE BEE HIVE HOTEL**
doubles (with shared bathrooms) from €80 room only. This very lovely hotel is American-owned and conveniently located near the Termini train station.
*Via Marghera 8*
*+39 06 447 04553*
*Website: the-beehive.com*

**RESIDENZA ZACELLINI**
doubles from €145 B&B
*Via Modena 5*
*+39 06 478 25204*
*Website: residenzacellini.it*

 **TRAVEL TIP** When you are booking a B&B— which clearly stands for Bed and Breakfast—you need to make sure that breakfast is actually included. Sometimes it isn't! Italians might call call it a B&B but not give you breakfast unless it's been agreed upon at the time of booking.

## Getting around Rome

Most international flights land at Leonardo da Vinci Airport (also called Flamicino). My suggestion is to fly Alitalia, which I consider not only the best Italian airline but one of the best in the world! You'll enjoy almost royal treatment and can learn about Italy before you arrive by watching instructional videos and reading the complimentary literature en route.

Rome Airport Shuttle runs a door-to-door shuttle at €15 per person (about 40 minutes into the city).

**Rome Metro Train System**—Rome is a bit like New York City, in that many of its residents move around by means of the metro. **Leonardo Express trains** leave every 30 minutes to the central train station, Roma Termini (35 minute trip). Be aware that these trains arrive at Platform 25, a quarter-mile walk from the main station. Tickets cost €14 online, €15 at the departure platform. If there are at least three in your party, it might be more convenient and cheaper to grab a cab, and you'll be delivered to your door. You can only buy a general ticket for a specific route (Termini), but it's good for any time. Get your ticket stamped in a yellow validation machine just before using it; the ticket will expire 90

### It's Criminal!

Do you want to know what's considered a real crime in Italy? Asking your barista or bartender (or whatever you want to call that kind man behind the counter in a coffee shop) to serve you a cappuccino at lunch or in the afternoon!

Especially in Rome, Italians consume a cappuccino with a croissant—the usual Italian breakfast—only in the morning. If you order a cappuccino in the afternoon or with lunch, most likely you will be looked at strangely! For Italians, cappuccino after 11 am is a big no-no!

By the way, Italians call a coffee shop a bar. Yes, Italian bars are not like American bars. In fact, they are only open during the daytime, though they can serve alcohol all day long, even for breakfast.

minutes after validation. If you don't get your ticket validated, you will be fined.

The **Metropolitan train** doesn't stop at Termini. Get off at Tiburtina Station or, before that, at Ostiense Station, where you can connect to Line B of the Rome Metro, or get off at Trastevere Station and from there take the '8' tram (direction 'Argentina') to go to Largo Argentina and Campo de' Fiori. Tickets are €8, plus €1 for a metro/tram ticket. The extra cost of the Leonardo Express is for the convenience of a direct ride to Termini. If you are going somewhere else close to a Metro station, Tiburtina and Ostiense stations are just as convenient. Get your ticket stamped in a yellow validation machine just before using it.

**Buses and trams**—I recommend taking a "hop-on hop-off" double-decker bus tour to get a closer view of the Eternal City, at least on your first day. Look for one with a drop-off and pick-up spot close to your hotel, and open seating on top so you can take plenty of photos. For details, check viator.com; you can even buy your tickets online.

There are hundreds of regular bus and tram lines running from 5:30 am until midnight and more than 20 night bus lines (marked with an owl) that run from 12:30 to 5:30 am. You can purchase tickets on board. All buses and trams travel in both directions. The main terminal stations are Termini (Piazza dei Cinquecento) and Piazza Venezia.

*The tram adds some modernity to a picturesque Roman street.*

In an effort to minimize pollution in the small back streets of the historic center, the city has established several electric bus lines to navigate alleyways barely wide enough for a Vespa.

**Rome on Two Wheels**—If you remember, the actors in *Roman Holiday* scoot around the city on an Italian Vespa motorcycle. You can rent the same kind of motorcycle and ride around with your loved one, just like Audrey Hepburn and Gregory Peck. However, it is truly important to pay attention to where you are going, as many motorcycle accidents happen each year in Rome.

To really "do as the Romans do" and ride around on a Vespa, you can find rental places all around the city; average rates are €40 to €50 per day. One of the best places is Rent Scooter Borgo S.a.S. at Via delle Grazie 2 (phone 0039 06 6877239—but if you're in Rome you don't have to use the 0039-06 area code).

*A Vespa motor scooter is the classic and fun way to see Rome the way the Romans do.*

*Roman metro stations are clean and modern.*

## ON LOCATION ROME

MOVIE: *When in Rome*
RELEASE: **2010**
DIRECTOR: **Mark Steven Johnson**
CAST: **Kristen Bell, Josh Duhamel**

This is another funny film about love, and of course Rome. I'm sure you've heard the old saying, "Throw a coin in the fountain and you might find love." Well, that's what is at the center of this comedy.

Kristen Bell plays the role of Beth, a workaholic young woman from New York, single and attractive. She is invited by her younger sister to be maid of honor for her wedding in Rome. She has no intention of getting hitched, but once she arrives in the city of eternal love, that lovebird starts calling her name. To upend the old myth about throwing coins in the fountain, she does the opposite and starts picking them out of the water—not realizing that a sort of spell will connect her to the men who've lost hope of finding the woman of their dreams. She'll be stalked by these guys, until she meets Nick, played by Josh Duhamel. (By the way, ladies, I had the pleasure of singing in front of Josh and his beautiful wife, Fergie, and I can tell you that he is really beautiful and intense!)

*During the scene in which Beth picks up the coins, she enters the water with a bottle of champagne in hand. After a drunken speech, she looks up and motions toward the statue, holding the bottle in her left hand. The bottle disappears when she turns around, then inexplicably reappears on the edge of the fountain when she starts grabbing coins from the water.*

This is definitely a chick flick, but probably many of you men reading this book have watched it, making your girlfriends and wives happy! By the way, my favorite song from the movie is Jason Mraz singing "Kickin with You"—really nice!

The plot of the film is the reverse of the 1954 movie *Three Coins in the Fountain*, about women who throw coins in a fountain and find love. Jean Negulesco directed that film, which starred Clifton Webb, Dorothy McGuire, Jean Peters, Louis Jourdan, Rossano Brazzi, and Maggie McNamara.

## What was filmed in Rome?

I am sorry to let you down, but with the exception of an aerial shot and cameras rolling briefly on Rome's most famous attractions (such as the Roman Forum), only the scenes at the Fountain of Love were actually shot in Rome. In fact, much of the film takes place in New York City. Also, when Beth travels to Rome to attend the wedding of her sister Joan, and when Beth returns to Rome for her own wedding. The Fountain of Love was inspired by the Trevi Fountain, but in reality it was a prop constructed about a third of a mile north of the Pantheon.

On a side note, I would love to make a point about so many American movies shot in Italy. It's funny to see how frequently they stereotype Italians and insist on showing Italy in a way that's much more like it was as far back as the 1950s. Dancing that kind of tarantella, at a marriage in Rome? Unfortunately, I don't think that will ever happen! Most young people hire a DJ and it's pretty much all American music. Also, the tarantella is from southern Italy—it's not part of Roman tradition at all. With that said, I still think *When in Rome* is a sweet movie that will put you in the mood for love.

*Beth's sister says that for the spell to be broken, Beth must be the one to put the coins back in the fountain; she can't just mail them back to Rome. But at the end of the movie, it's Nick and not Beth who throws the poker chip into the water—yet the spell is broken anyway. Are we going to have* When in Rome 2: the Revenge?

## ON LOCATION ROME

MOVIE: *To Rome with Love*
RELEASE: 2012
DIRECTOR: **Woody Allen**
CAST: **Woody Allen, Roberto Benigni, Judy Davis, Alec Baldwin, Ellen Page, Penelope Cruz, Jesse Eisenberg**

In the last few years, Woody Allen has brought his iconic movies to Europe. *To Rome with Love* follows four different characters and their dramas—a well-known American architect reliving his youth, an average middle-class Roman who turns into a celebrity, a young married woman drawn into an affair, and an American opera director endeavoring to put a singing funeral director on stage. It all takes place in Rome.

The director wanted to show areas that aren't the same old locations seen in so many other movies. He focused a lot on Sant'Angelo (page 54), Garbatella, and Rione Monti. Allen also shot some scenes in Piazza del Popolo (page 59) and Campo dei Fiori. Let's take a look at the areas we haven't already visited.

**La Garbatella**—*Garbato* means "polite, amiable." The suffix *ella* adds a bit of gracefulness and a female reference. The general opinion is that this area's name referred to an innkeeper who provided refreshments to pilgrims and workers at the Basilica San Paolo.

This neighborhood is no tourist area. Garbatella is south of the main historic sites, the Pyramid of Cestius, and the Ostiense train station. Look for the "gasometro" gas storage facility and continue south another half mile, or take the metro to Garbatella and walk southeast for a few minutes. Twisting, climbing streets and odd but interesting postmodern-looking buildings will tell you that you've arrived.

**Rione Monti**—Monti is the name of one of Rome's twelve *rioni*, or wards; the name *Monti* means mountains, from the fact that the Esquiline and Viminal hills, and parts of the Quirinal and Caelian hills, belong to this rione. This neighborhood in the historic heart of Rome spreads along Via Panisperna between the Roman Forum and Piazza della Madonna dei Monti.

Densely populated in ancient days and turned rather seedy over succeeding years, Rione Monti today is a lively traditional working-class neighborhood with an increasingly young and arty vibe. You'll find restaurants and cafés, wine bars, grocery stores and a marketplace, international bookstores, and a cinema.

Restaurant choices include the century-old **La Carbonara** (Via Panisperna 214), typical Roman cuisine including a choice of handmade pasta; the refined **Il Covo** (Via del Boschetto 91), classic cuisine; **Trattoria Luzzi** (Via di San Giovanni 88 in Laterano), typical Roman cuisine and pizza; and **La Cicala e la Formica** (Via Leonina 17), candlelight and classical cuisine. For pizza, there's **La Vecchia Roma** (Via Leonina 10) or **Le Carrette** (Vicolo delle Carrette 14).

**Al Vino al Vino** (Via dei Serpenti 19) and **Cavour 313** (Via Cavour 313) are wine bars offering hundreds of Italian and international wines. For nightlife, check out **Oppio Caffé** (Via delle Terme di Tito 72), American-style bar and restaurant; **Shamrock** (Via del Colosseo 1/C,), Celtic and Irish music; and **Charity Caffé** (Via Panisperna 68), live jazz music.

And if you're looking for reading material, head to **Feltrinelli** (Via V.E. Orlando 84/86) or **Mel Bookstore** (Via Nazionale 254/255).

**Campo dei Fiori**—This rectangular square south of Piazza Navona is known for its vibrant open-air farmers' market, restaurants, and lively nightlife. The onetime meadow—Campo dei Fiori means "Field of Flowers"—was the site of public executions some centuries back, and a statue of philosopher Giordano Bruno, burned for heresy in 1600, dominates the square. Consider staying at this romantic, ivy-covered boutique hotel:

**HOTEL CAMPO DE' FIORI**
*Via del Biscione 6, 00186 Roma*
**Website:** *hotelcampodefiori.com*

## ON LOCATION ROME

MOVIE: *Eat Pray Love*
RELEASE: 2010
DIRECTOR: Ryan Murphy
CAST: Julia Roberts, Javier Bardem,
  Richard Jenkins, James Franco

I loved this movie! Romantic, yes, but with some true soul-searching. How many of us have wondered if the life we are living is truly filling our sense of completion? How many times have we asked ourselves, "Is this the place where I belong? Is this the person of my life? What is my true calling and mission?"

Well, this is the kind of movie that frees you completely and encourages you to embrace the good that life can bring, even if that means putting everything on the line in the name of love and happiness. Julia Roberts plays the role of a woman (Liz) who needs to abandon all that is around her and challenge herself by traveling for a year around the world,

*The book* Eat, Pray, Love *by Elizabeth Gilbert was listed as a favorite of Oprah Winfrey. That led to Julia Roberts' interest in the book and her optioning the rights to make a film of it.*

encountering new cultures, new relationships, and new places in order to find solace in her soul and peace of mind. The first stop? Rome, of course!

So let's see where her romantic path led her. Of course, we see her visiting the Colosseum (page 55). Julia in the movie also finds some relaxation at **Villa Borghese**. The beautiful

*The Villa Borghese is home to an art museum and beautiful, peaceful gardens.*

Borghese Gardens, reaching from above Piazza del Popolo to the top of Via Veneto north of the city's center, are a great place to get away from the hustle and bustle of Rome. It's hard to believe you are still in the city when you're inside this vast park. The 17th-century Villa Borghese itself is now an art museum. You can get there easily by hopping on metro Line A and getting off at the Flaminio station.

Liz (Julia) suffers from a bad romantic breakup and finds strange consolation by visiting the **Mausoleum of Augustus**. When built in 26 BC, the massive tomb of the emperor was among the most remarkable monuments of Rome. The inner tomb once held the ashes

*The ruins of the Mausoleum of Augustus are all that remains of one of the most impressive buildings of the ancient world.*

of Augustus (who died in 14 AD) and his wife Livia; an outer ring contained the urns of other members of the imperial family. This is definitely an important part of Roman Empire history to visit, though it suffered from looting and neglect over the centuries and wire fencing now prevents access. • **Piazza Augusto Imperatore** (corner Via di Ripetta); next to the modern museum building housing the Ara Pacis, the altar to the Roman goddess of peace consecrated in 9 BC.

Going back to Liz's relaxing moments in *Eat Pray Love*, she enjoys a gelato while sitting by the magnificent **Trevi Fountain** (page 50). Isn't it amazing how many directors have chosen this majestic sculpture to bring magic to their movies? The movie also takes Liz to another ancient and marvelous place, full of traditions: the beautiful city of Naples. Turn to the following chapter to see where she ate pizza in Napoli!

## PIZZA MARGHERITA a la *Eat Pray Love*

As I have shared with you, in this movie Julia Roberts' character decides to immerse herself in the fantastic world of "true Italian food." I already unveiled the secret location, the famous Italian pizzeria where the best pizza can be found and devoured, just like Julia did in this movie, right here at *L 'Antica Pizzeria da Michele* in the heart of Naples. But I would love for you to learn to how to make this delicious dish, called **Pizza Margherita**. It is a very simple recipe to make:

### PIZZA MARGHERITA

**For the dough:**

150 grams of 00 flour

150 grams of all-purpose flour

4 teaspoons of dry yeast

Half a spoon of olive oil

(Of course you can buy the dough already made at the grocery store if you don't have the patience to make it. However, once you make your own dough the first time, you are going to love it!)

**For the toppings:**

2 large full spoons of tomato sauce (remember to season it as you please before spreading it all over the dough)

Some fresh mozzarella in water (preferably cherry mozzarella)

Some basil

Extra virgin olive oil

Salt, pepper, and a dash of sugar (if desired, but not necessary)

### Preparation (for 2 people)

In a large bowl, combine the flour and salt. In a separate bowl, mix a cup of warm water, the yeast, and olive oil. Add this mixture to the flour. Let the dough rest for five minutes. After that, cut the ball in two pieces, place them on two different plates, and cover them with a dampened cloth. Let them rise for at least 3 hours.

When ready, find a work station where you can spread some flour (to prevent the dough from sticking to the surface) and lay down the dough. Use your hands "Italian style" (I don't really mean make the dough fly up in the air, but your hands can help the dough stretch in preparation for laying on the baking pan). After the dough is ready on the pan, add a spoonful of olive oil and two spoonfuls of tomato sauce, which you will want to spread all across and on top of the stretched dough. After laying the sauce, sprinkle on top a large quantity of mozzarella. I know that in America shredded mozzarella is commonly used. But I suggest you try fresh mozzarella in water, better known as "cherry mozzarella" ( small balls of fresh mozzarella in water). Deposit the cheese with care on top of the pizza and then add some more tomato sauce, which you should season as you prefer. I usually use a sprinkle of salt, some pepper, and a dash of sugar to kill a bit of the tomato's acidity. Finally, drizzle olive oil once again on top of the pizza and add some basil on top.

Bake at 500 degrees for about 5–7 minutes, or at least until the crust is golden. Do not leave it in the oven too long as it can become extremely hard to eat or, even worse, burn!

Here's another delicious recipe from *Eat Pray Love* that you can make at home:

**Eggs, Asparagus, Italian Ham (prosciutto):** Roberts' character, Liz, decides to stay home only for one day and embrace the old Italian saying "Il Dolce Far Niente," which means "the sweet doing nothing." So she prepares a delicious and fast snack. She drizzles olive oil over some inviting fresh asparagus, hard boiled eggs, and prosciutto, and pours herself a glass of Italian red wine—how satisfying and delicious!

# 8

# Naples, its Coast, and its Islands

*"To my mind, the greatest reward and luxury of travel is to be able to experience everyday things as if for the first time, to be in a position in which almost nothing is so familiar it is taken for granted."* —BILL BRYSON

## NAPLES

Naples is a favorite destination for Italians, especially during summer. Not only is this city full of music, history, killer food, and great sights, but it connects you to the most stunning islands in the world: Capri, Anacapri, Ischia, and Amalfi. En route to Naples from Rome, the coastal town of Sabaudia makes a perfect seaside interlude.

*The beach in Sabaudia is highly popular, but don't let the people distract you from the natural beauty.*

## Sabaudia

The beach at Sabaudia is long (about 12 miles), with beautiful fine sand and lots of seashells. The blue Tyrrhenian Sea is unusually clean here.

Sabaudia was completed in 1934. This is one of several towns built by Benito Mussolini (the Fascist dictator of Italy from 1922 to 1943) on the

reclaimed Pontine Marshes. Mussolini's efforts left central Italy with several new beach towns, along with farmland filled in autumn with grapes and zucchini. In a huge mosaic at the entrance to the Church of the Holy Annunciation in Sabaudia, Mussolini is shown gathering wheat (which he actually did).

The Sabaudia beach is easily identifiable, thanks to Mount Circeo jutting into the sea. The 1,775-foot-high headland is said to resemble the face of a sleeping woman whose hair is falling into the sea; some stories say it's the face of the sorceress Circe, who, abandoned by Odysseus, fell asleep and turned into a mountain. Mount Circeo and this coastline are part of

Circeo National Park. Many Italian directors have filmed here, including comedian and director Alberto Sordi and director Federico Fellini.

In summer the beach is always very crowded, especially on weekends. It has become "famous" in recent years due to the presence of numerous VIPs from the worlds of politics and show biz. Nighttime along this coast is simply superb. You can even swim in the sea at night; the water is warm and the moonlight creates a spectacle

### MOVIES

Eat Pray Love
The Talented Mr. Ripley

of light on water. For dining, the **Trattoria il Grottino** in San Felice Circeo (just below Sabaudia) naturally specializes in seafood. My group found the mussels in black pepper sauce sweet (the mussels) and tangy (the delicious sauce), the pasta with seafood excellent, and the *filetto di sogliola alla mugnaia* (filet of sole meuniere) perfectly cooked and tasting fresh from the sea. This is a pretty expensive restaurant, but worth it. • 2 Piazza Vittorio Veneto, 04017 San Felice Circeo; phone +39 0773 548446.

Sabaudia is about 62 miles southeast of Rome, supposedly an hour's drive—but it took us nearly two hours because of weather and rush-hour traffic. If you are traveling by road,

*The Veiled Christ is a masterpiece of delicate technique.*

the movie *Eat Pray Love*, I can assure you that this is one of the most gorgeous cities in all of Italy. Naples is the capital of the Campania region.

In the historic center of the city, the carved marble figure of the *Veiled Christ* at **Sansevero Chapel** often elicits comments such as "the statue seems to come to life." Sculpted in 1753 by Giuseppe Sanmartino, the figure of Christ lies under what looks like the thinnest of fabrics. The facial features, body, and even the crucifixion wounds are clearly visible beneath the delicate folds of the marble "veil." The visual effect is truly stunning. Many other 18th-century artworks are also displayed in the chapel (museosansevero.it). • Via Francesco De Sanctis 19, 80135 Naples, phone +39 081 5518470; open weekdays 10 am–5:40 pm (closed Tuesdays), Sundays 10 am–1:10 pm.

Rome isn't the only ancient city with an underground world to explore. Beneath the medieval church of **San Lorenzo Maggiore** in the heart of Naples, you'll find the excavated remains of a first-century Roman market.

Unlike the Roman Forum, where you really have to use your imagination to picture what the streets and buildings once looked like, here you

*The underground ruins of a Roman market offer the adventurous traveler a chance to experience the ancient world close up.*

leave in plenty of time to avoid getting stuck in traffic!

## Naples

Napoli is the true city of the heart! Although it had a more minor presence than Rome in see storefronts with walls and ceilings intact. What's more, you can walk into the "rooms" to get a peek at the Roman laundry (one basin for washing, another for rinsing) and bakery (the bread oven looks essentially like today's pizza ovens in Naples). There are Greek ruins here, too. The whole thing gives you chills—and not just because it's downright cold underground. Visit sanlorenzomaggiorenapoli. it to learn more. • Piazza San Gaetano 316 (off Via dei Trubunali), 80138 Napoli, phone +39 081 2110860; open Monday–Saturday from 9:30 am to 5:30 pm, Sunday from 9:30 am to 1:30 pm.

The city's **National Archaeological Museum** houses one of the most remarkable collections of Roman art and artifacts in the world. Among its displays are massive fresco and mosaic panels, sculptures, and other objects taken from Pompeii and Herculaneum. • Piazza Museo 19, 80135 Naples, phone +39 081 4422149; open Wednesday–Monday, 9 am to 8 pm.

You absolutely want to take a day trip to the **ancient city of Pompeii** and neighboring Herculaneum. Pompeii was destroyed in 79 AD by the eruption of Mount Vesuvius, 5 miles away. Thousands of children, women, and men were burned alive and buried under volcanic ash—remaining undiscovered for 1,500 years. You can see this amazing testament to history by taking one of the frequent trains or buses that go to the excavated site from Naples, or by driving on the A3. Pompeii is just southeast of Naples at the modern suburban town of Pompei (with a single "i").

 Naples is a splendid city, but few people here speak English. Make sure you have your electronic translator with you—or plan ahead and take an Italian course (I recommend Rosetta Stone).

*This statue of the Greek hero Hercules, also in the National Archaeological Museum, is one of the most celebrated sculptures in history.*

*The Farnese Bull, located in Naples's National Archaeological Museum, is the largest single sculpture that has survived from antiquity.*

*This portrait of a young, upwardly mobile middle-class couple was recovered from the ruins of Pompeii. Amazingly, we actually know the name of the man in the portrait, Terentius Neo, and his profession—he owned a bakery.*

*The ruins of a public building in Pompeii, open to travelers.*

## Getting to Naples

Naples is 140 miles southeast of Rome, 480 miles from Milan, and 450 miles from Venice. Alibus Airport Shuttle runs between the Naples airport, the central train station (Piazza Garibaldi), and Molo Beverello Port.

**Arriving by air**—Naples International Airport provides connections to international destinations and all other Italian airports. The airport is 4 miles from the central rail station in the Capodichino district of the city.

**Arriving by train**—You can get to Naples by rail from throughout Italy. The principal train station is Napoli Centrale at Piazza Garibaldi, to the east of the old city. Trains run directly between Rome's main train station, Roma Termini, and Napoli Centrale all day long, from about 5 am until about 10:15 pm. You can check schedules and ticket prices at Trenitalia.com. These are the options from Rome:

- *Rapido (R) and Regional*— The least expensive and slowest alternative (nearly three hours), Rapido trains offer second-class seating, and no reserved seats.

- *IC and ICplus*—Intercity and Intercity Plus trains take just over two hours, with first and second-class compartments and seat reservations available. Cost is almost double the lowest rapido fare, but since the trains can be crowded, having a seat reservation is a good idea.

- *ESA or ESfast*—Eurostar trains take less than two hours, have first and second-class compartments, and require seat reservations. These cost about triple the lowest rapido fares. Note: some Eurostar trains go to other stations than Centrale.

---

### Make Mine a Double

The best pizza in the world is what you see when Julia Roberts' character in the movie *Eat Pray Love* (page 70) goes to the center of Naples. The pizzeria is called **L'Antica Pizzeria da Michele**, and if you really want to go to pizza heaven, you must try their famous Margherita pizza with double mozzarella. It is really to die for!

To reach Julia's pizza nirvana, you can take the subway to the Piazza Garibaldi stop, direction Corso Umberto/Piazza Bovio; the pizzeria is less than a half-mile away. You can also go by bus on the main line from Piazza Municipio. Past Piazza Nicola Amore (also known as the four buildings), you'll see a red corner building. The road to your left leads to the pizzeria. • Via Cesare Sersale 1, 80139 Naples; website damichele.net; phone 081 5539204.

**Arriving by road**—The A1 (Autostrada del Sole) connects Naples with Rome and beyond, all the way to Milan. The drive from Rome takes less than two hours. The A3 goes from Naples southeast to Salerno and continues on to the toe of Italy. The A16 links Naples with Avellino, continuing across the Italian boot to meet the A14 and the Adriatic coast.

## The Coast and Islands

About 35 miles southeast of Naples, the village of **Sant'Agata sui Due Golfi** marks the start of the Amalfi Coast road (SS145). Before the road was built in the mid-19th century on the orders of the Bourbon ruler Ferdinand II, the coastal hamlets were accessible only by boat or mule-track. **Punta Campanella** divides the Gulf of Naples from the Gulf of Salerno. The seas here are where Ulysses met the Sirens (this Ulysses got around, huh?)—a magical place to visit by land or sea, a place to immerse yourself in raw beauty and poetry.

To me, renting a car and driving is the best way to enjoy this region. Driving along the twisting Amalfi Coast road is like something out of a fairy tale. The road to Sorrento, Positano, Amalfi, and Ravello offers enchantingly beautiful views: be sure to stop every so often to enjoy the perfumes and colors of the Mediterranean.

And just 40 minutes by boat from Naples, you can experience pure paradise on earth—the Neapolitan islands. Visiting the islands is an experience you should have at least once in your lifetime.

My favorite is the trip to **Ischia**, the largest island in the Gulf of Naples. Along with historical and art treasures waiting for you to discover, it has excellent natural hot springs, thanks to its volcanic origins. The main harbor is simply an old crater filled with seawater. The water surrounding the island is emerald green in color.

The island of **Capri** is just 3 nautical miles beyond the protected maritime area off Punta Campanella. Chic and worldly but with timeless appeal, Capri is the site of the extraordinary Blue Grotto (Grotta Azzurra). Washed in brilliant blue light, the sea cave can be explored by boat.

## Getting to the Islands

If you want to do some island-hopping (a bit like going from island to island in Hawaii), little ferries—*traghetti*—depart from Naples every day, all day long, for Catania, Palermo, Cagliari, Capri, Ischia, Procida, the Aeolian Islands, the Egadi islands, and the Pontine islands. It's a gorgeous and fun boat ride. Molo Beverello is the main ferry port. Others are Mergellina and Pozzuoli.

My suggestion is to buy your ticket online and arrive at least 35 minutes before boarding time, to avoid a long line of people pushing you back and forth (Italians are very animated people). You can also buy tickets right at the port, but I have to warn you that it's always super-crowded, especially in summer (the perfect time to go). Look for the Angelino castle in front of the port of Naples and then a square building where *I Biglietti* are sold—the tickets to hop onto your ferry. The cost is around €15 per person, depending on how much luggage you have; try to travel light when you visit the islands.
• Ok-ferry bookings: <u>ok-ferry.com</u>.

## Where to Stay
### DON ALFONSO 1890

I try my best to find unique places for you to visit. Thanks

*Capri's Blue Grotto is an otherworldy and unforgettable experience.*

*Approaching the island of Ischia from the sea. What a view!*

to my Avis car and our Italian coordinator, Ludovico Mandiello, my team found the most welcoming, charming, and luscious hotel in the heart of the Sorrentine Peninsula at Sant'Agata.

I was curious to see what everyone had been talking about. I expected another beautiful hotel with elegant amenities, but perhaps a bit cold, as such places sometimes are. This is a question I sometimes get: Romina, where can we find an amazing place with a warmth that makes us feel taken care of in every detail, embraced? Well, I have a feeling you've just found it!

In 1890, Alfonso Costanzo Iaccarino—grandfather of the present-day Alfonso—returned to his native Italy after spending several years in America. He came to this spot and began what would one day become one of the best-known restaurants in the world. But let's get right into it, starting with the warm welcome by the staff (mom Livia, son, and father, their relatives and employees). Don Alfonso 1890 is a true home, and you feel it right away as you walk through the library, with its luscious silk tapestries, soft couches, beautiful rugs, and elegant fireplace. You see it in the artwork, flowers and fruits, colors and scents that make you realize you are truly in the heart of Italy.

I was given the most beautiful suite, and I felt like a princess, or maybe a Barbie doll; the colors in the room were enticing, seducing, very

**TRAVEL TIP** Every great metropolis will have its share of thieves, so make sure to have your belongings where other hands can't reach them. Don't wear expensive jewelry when you are on the boat or waiting to board—you could attract the attention of the wrong people. Try to blend in, without calling attention to yourself. Once you're seated on board, just enjoy the ride!

*My bedroom at the Don Alfonso. Don't those beds look inviting?*

*Peering into the world-famous, 25,000-bottle wine cellar. You begin in a 17th-century Neapolitan building, which then leads to an earlier wing from the 16th century. After descending about 40 meters into the earth, you'll find yourself in what used to be a 6th century Etruscan tomb! And it is right at the bottom of the tomb that the Iaccarini family age some of their incredible cheeses.*

with a flavor and scent that make you want to drink the entire bottle—with unfortunate consequences for people like me who aren't used to drinking but consider liqueur a dessert. But that's another story.)

It was like being a **bambina** again when Livia collected me and my team and said she wanted to take us on a wild ride into their farm. It's important to her for people to know that every single fruit and vegetable is treated with the utmost care, as are the animals. She swears that if you talk nicely to a cow you'll get better milk and cheese.

So here we were, running about in a little utility car in the center of this gorgeous organic farm, La Peracciola, built along the water. The lemons and tomatoes are so fresh and juicy that you can taste them as you pick them. Ah—the sweet taste of Italy! Now I've really experienced the true nature of my country.

Southern with pink, golden, white, blue—the hues of the Mediterranean. And though I was there for business and needed to stay neutral to the pleasures surrounding me, I just couldn't help myself. I am in love with this place! My suite had a huge terrace overlooking Sant'Agata and the coast. I didn't want to leave that room. It was pure luxury, from the bed linens to the large, modern Jacuzzi and inviting shower.

There are only eight suites, and you cannot have a wrong one—they are all fantastic. If you've ever wanted to live the life of the rich and famous, this five-star hotel is the place to do it. If you're getting married, this is where to hold your wedding so that your guests will never forget it.

Livia, the wife of Alfonso and the true "queen" of the hotel, is a beautiful and elegant woman

who is also very down to earth. To me, she will always remain the best hotelier I have ever met. I love her! She cherishes the people who visit her. This is a woman who comes, even in the rain, to offer you their famous lemon liqueur. (This is something extremely delicate,

*Marvelous things happen in the Don Alfonso kitchen.*

Who could have known that I had to go to the Amalfi Coast to do so, to experience the sane and wholesome life that keeps people healthy—and with unbelievable skin! It must truly be the olive oil.

Now I know the meaning of touching heaven. We were lucky to get to explore the farm, which isn't always open to guests. Be sure to request an appointment if you want the tour.

**Cooking school.** Alfonso's son Iaccarini is a talented chef who runs a cooking school right in the hotel. You can join in hands-on preparation of foods indigenous to the Sorrento Peninsula, from handmade ravioli to smoked mozzarella zucchini puffs. Each day's class features a different theme: seasonal vegetables, seafood, fresh pasta, meats, or *dolci*.

Hotel guests can also take part in a unique wine tasting, sampling wines kept in cellars that date back to pre-Roman times.

If you think this is the first book to talk about the Don Alfonso 1890 experience, think again! I was surprised to see on their shelves a myriad of books with Don Alfonso as the main subject—and no, the family didn't commission them (except for one cookbook by Don Alfonso himself). Writers from all over the world have come here because this combination of museum, culinary school, and farm gives them plenty to write about.

**Bookings.** Don Alfonso 1890 is pretty much always booked up, so you need to make your reservations well in advance. Daily rates are €300 to €650, depending on the season.

## LA BECCACCIA

One Ischia hotel in particular took me by surprise with its design and location. This marvelous family-owned hotel/resort/village/restaurant (with its own farm, too!) offers practically anything you might want, from water sports to

---

**DON ALFONSO 1890**
*Corso S. Agata 11*
*80064 S. Agata Sui Due*
*Golfi (Campania)*
**Phone :** + 39 081 8780026
**Website:** donalfonso.com

Here are some other fine hotels and restaurants along the Amalfi Coast and on the Neapolitan islands:

**ALBERGO
SAN MONTANO**
*Via Nuova Montevico 26*
*80076 Lacco Ameno*
  *(Ischia)*
**Phone:** +39 081 994033
**Website:** sanmontano.com

**BELLEVUE SYRENE**
Two centuries of hospitality in Sorrento.
*Piazza della Vittoria 5*
*80067 Sorrento*
**Phone:** +39 081 8781024
**Website:** bellevue.it

**BLU CAPRI RELAIS**
Mediterranean design in Anacapri.
*Via Giuseppe Orlandi 103*
*80071 Anacapri*
**Phone:** +39 081 8373924
**Website:** www.relaisblu.com

**CAESAR AUGUSTUS**
That view! That pool!
Those suites!
*Via Giuseppe Orlandi 4*
*80071 Anacapri*
**Phone:** +39 081 8373395
**Website:** caesar-augustus.
  com

## Romina's Hotel Picks

**CAPRI TIBERIO PALACE
HOTEL & SPA**
At home with the emperor.
*Via Croce 11-15*
*80073 Capri*
**Phone:** +39 081 9787111
**Website:** tiberiopalace.
  com

**LA BECCACCIA**
*Via Cava Scialicco 1*
*80075 Forio (NA), Ischia*
**Phone:** +39 081 994510
**Website:** www.hotel
ristorantelabeccaccia
  ischia.it

nighttime entertainment to three gigantic blue swimming pools. My suite had a huge patio directly overlooking the water, with stairs going all the way down into the thermal area—simply beautiful! (If a wedding's in your future, La Beccaccia would be the perfect romantic frame for an engagement party or wedding reception.)

The suites are designed as adorable little Italian cottages, with their own patios looking onto the water. The bedrooms are very comfortable, with pretty hard mattresses—old school Italian, I should say. I guess they are good for your back! The food is to die for, and the staff is so warm and friendly; they'll go out of their way to make your vacation unforgettable.

Ask to be taken to the thermal waters at nighttime, down a long stairway built in the rocks, to bathe in the warm natural bubbles. It is truly out of this world, swimming in the warm water at night with the moon as your best friend, keeping you company and shining its silver light upon you.

The name La Beccaccia means "The Angry Bird"—don't ask me why. When we arrived, they showed us a stuffed bird. From the look on his face, I thought he must have been pretty angry. Poor bird. Most likely they will show it to you, too—Italians are so proud of things like that.

## Ischia

Ischia is a fun island known for its thermal waters and sea-ori-

## ON LOCATION NEAPOLITAN ISLANDS

MOVIE: *The Talented Mr. Ripley*
RELEASE: **1999**
DIRECTOR: **Anthony Minghella**
CAST: **Matt Damon, Jude Law, Gwyneth Paltrow**

Now let's check out one of my favorite movies ever: *The Talented Mr. Ripley*. Tom Ripley (Matt Damon) is a young con artist who pretends to be the friend of a rich man's son and gets paid $1,000 to fly to Italy to convince Dickie Greenleaf (Jude Law), the son, to return home to the United States. But when Tom meets Dickie's girlfriend, Marge (Gwyneth Paltrow), and experiences the life of the privileged son, he doesn't want to give up the beautiful things that can come to him now. He goes to extreme lengths to have it all, with terrible consequences.

*A few scenes filmed in Rome weren't acceptable to the the producers and director, so the Roman set was built all over again in New York to refilm the scenes.*

### On Ischia Island
The Italian connection starts when Ripley arrives at the Palermo airport in Sicily to track down Dickie. But this movie was shot largely on Ischia, biggest of the three volcanic islands in the Bay of Naples.

To represent the fictitious resort of Mongibello (where Dickie meets his girlfriend), the director divided the shooting between Ischia and the gorgeous island of Procida. (You can do your own island hopping with Ferry OK—see page 77 for details.)

*Tom Ripley presents Marge with a bottle of perfume from Santa Maria Novella—the same perfumer used by Hannibal Lecter in the 2001 movie* Hannibal. *The store where Ripley sees Dickie's initials is actually a Gucci store on Via Condotti in Rome.*

*Dickie, his friend Fausto, and Tom sing a funny song titled "Tu Vuò Fà L'Americano." This was an actual successful song in the 1950s, and the Italian man who played the role of Fausto is Rosario Fiorelllo, an Italian television showman known for his comedy and imitations of well-known singers. I've appeared on national Italian television with him a couple of times; he is a wonderful Sicilian fellow and extremely talented.*

The Castello Aragonese was originally built in the fourth century BC by Hiero, the Greek tyrant of Syracuse in Sicily. Later fortifications and the stone bridge were added in the fifteenth century AD by Alfonso V, the Spanish king of Naples.

ented vacations, but there is much more to explore here. The best way to get around is by walking or renting a bicycle, but you can also rent a car or use the public transportation system, which works wonderfully. Summertime is definitely the best time to visit the island (even though it's filled with tourists then), as you'll want to take a luxuriating swim.

The ferry will take you to Ischia's main port, **Ischia Porto**, but the place where Ripley gets off the bus (see the box below) is **Ischia Ponte**, below the towering 12th-century **Aragonese Castle**. Dominating the island's northeast coast, the castle rises on volcanic rock about a mile east of the ferry landing and is connected by regular bus service. Built in 474 BC by Hiero I of Syracuse, over the centuries the fortress has been occupied by the Parthenopeans (the ancient inhabitants of Naples), Romans, French, English, and Bourbons. A stone causeway was built in about 1440 to connect it to the main island. Privately owned since 1912, Aragonese Castle is Ischia's most-visited attraction.

## Irpinia

I'd also love for you to explore the magnificent area called Irpinia. Part of the Appenine Mountains around the very pretty town of Avellino, about 25 miles east of Naples, Irpinia is

*A breathtaking view in Irpinia.*

Actor Anthony Quinn sampling the hospitality of the O'pagliarone restaurant.

**TRAVEL TIP**

**For Further Details...**

For further information about the Naples area, you can contact the following. (Dial 011-39 first if calling from overseas.)

• Azienda Autonoma di Soggiorno, Cura e Turismo di Napoli (Autonomous Local Tourist Office of the City of Naples)
*Via San Carlo 9*
*80100 Napoli*
*Phone: +39 081 402394*
Website: www.inaples.it/eng/

a well-known, very productive region. As noted earlier, it is also the birthplace of legendary director Sergio Leone.

One of the area's best dining spots is **O'pagliarone**. The walls of the cozy and rustic restaurant are pratically covered with pictures of the stars (Italian and American) who have dined here. This was the favorite restaurant of late actor Anthony Quinn, and pictures of him with the late owner (father of the present owner) are pretty much everywhere. I found the food (made with the freshest organic ingredients) and service to be pure excellence! The food kept on coming—of course, that's true almost everywhere you go in Italy—and the ambiance felt so warm and happy. • Via Campi 3, 83024 Monteforte Irpino; phone +39 082 5753101.

Something to keep in mind if you are on a budget is that

The world-class pizza at O'pagliarone restaurant simply must be experienced!

there is a corporate bed and breakfast in Avellino operated as part of a large convention facility and cultural club. Called **Abacab**, it offers clean and affordable service. You just never know what will take you to Italy, even a business trip.
• Abacab, Via Nazionale 32 Monteforte Irpino.

**Did You Know?**
Franco Dragone, the musical creator of the Cirque du Soleil shows and Celine Dion's Las Vegas show *A New Day*, was born right here in the Irpinia region, in the town of Cairano.

## A Perfect Day In Napoli (Naples)

### Start your day with Caravaggio!

» The great artist Caravaggio spent only a few years in Naples, however he left us an incredible artistic legacy. Caravaggio became famous in Rome in the 1590s for being an unconventional artist who produced incredibly detailed paintings. After killing a young playboy in Rome in a duel, he fled for his life, hiding away as authorities decided to put him to death. What was the perfect place to hide? Naples, of course! You can view some of Caravaggio's amazing work at the **Capodimonte museum**.

*Capodimonte museum*
*Porta Piccola Via Miano 2, phone 081 749 9111*
*Transport Bus 24, 110, C57, C63, R4*
*Hours 8:30 am–7:30 pm Monday, Tuesday, and Thursday through Sunday (last entry is at 6:30 pm)*
*Admission €7.50; €6.50 after 2 pm; free under-18s, over-65s. Park free.*

» Or, if you have a taste for adventure, consider starting your day with a visit to **Pompeii and the Vesuvius volcanic sites.** Go to the Porta Marina entrance to the archaeological site and visit the main ticket office (081 857 5347, www. pompeiisites.org). Open Apr–Oct 8:30 am–6 pm daily, Nov–Mar 8:30 am–3:30 pm daily. The tourist offices at Pompeii also offer information on Torre del Greco, Torre Annunziata, and Castellammare di Stabia.

*The best way to get here to take the fast and comfortable train: All the main places to visit and sites are served by the* **Circumvesuviana railway** *(081 772 2444, www.vesuviana.it). If you're travelling from Naples to Pompeii, take the Naples–Sorrento line and get off at Pompeii Scavi–Villa dei Misteri. Trust me, this is a must!*

» Take a break with the real **espresso** and a **babà al rum**! Did you know that Naples is the city where the very first espresso was served? Yes indeed, in Naples there is a true coffee cult that you will not be able to find anywhere else in the world! So stop at one of the top coffee shops in all of Naples, **Gran Caffe' Aragonese**, and order a classic Neapolitan dessert called babà al rum, which is a small yeast cake "impregnated" in rum, and sometimes filled with whipped cream or pastry cream. It's so delish!

### Gran Caffé Aragonese
*Piazza San Domenico Maggiore 5/8, phone 081 552 8740*
*Transport Metro Museo or Piazza Cavour/bus CS, E1, R2*
*Open daily 7 am to midnight*

▶

## A Perfect Day continued

» If you have time you may want to check out some pretty amazing palaces and castles, so you can be queen or king at least for a day! You have to visit **Castel Nuovo**, located in Piazza del Municipio. Built in 1279 by Charles of Angiono, it today houses Naples' museo civico, with Neopolitan artworks spanning the 15th through 20th centuries. The Fortress Towers will make you feel like a real Royal.

*Castel Nuovo*
*Phone 081 795 5877, 081 420 1241*
*Transport Bus C25, R2, R3*
*Open 9am–7pm Mon-Sat; 9am–2.30pm Sun. Last entry one hour before closing.*
*Admission €5; free under-18s, over-65s.*

» And not too distant from Naples, and within reach simply by hopping on a little ferry from the city, you can get to the **Blue Grotto** (see page 76 for details) for the most romantic time. Phone 081 837 0973.

» **Best restaurant in Naples?** I have to admit, I had the best time in Naples and the food there is heavenly. But here it comes! **Da Donato dal 1956 Antica Trattoria e Pizzeria**. This is a very simple place, not fancy, but the food and prices are amazing!

*Da Donato dal 1956 Antica Trattoria e Pizzeria*
*Via Silvio Spaventa 41, phone 081287828.*

» Spend the **evening at the opera**. Are you looking for a bit of high culture? Then visit one of the most splendid opera houses in Naples, the **San Carlo theatre**, a magnificent, stunning building that is home to great classical entertainment.

*San Carlo theatre*
*Via San Carlo 98F, Royal Naples (in the heart of the city)*
*Phone 081 797 2331, 081 797 2412*
*Transport Bus 24, C22, C25, C57*
*Box office hours 10 am to 7 pm, Tuesday through Sunday*
*Performances times vary. Closed Aug.*
*Tickets €20–€250.*

# 9

# Sicily, the Hawaii of Italy

*"Live the life you love."* —Romina Arena

## SICILY

Sicily shines over and over again when it comes to movies. You have pretty much anything you might want here: sandy beaches, idyllic little villages and piazzas, delicious food, welcoming people, and even snow around Mount Etna. Sicily creates perfect movie sets, and that is why so many directors have chosen it as the "leading lady" for their films. Director Giuseppe Tornatore, for example, has used it as his own personal muse, to give life to his incredible stories in *Cinema Paradiso, Malèna,* and *Baaria.*

Sicily has a gigantic historical footprint. The Phoenicians, Greeks, Romans, Vandals, Arabs, Normans, and French have all left their marks in Sicily. That's why you will find Sicilians who are blonde with blue eyes, like Scandinavians, and others who have dark complexions and features, very Latin—it all comes from the combination of historic influences. There is no other place on earth where you can find all this incredible

### MOVIES

Cinema Paradiso
The Leopard
Il Postino
Malèna
The Godfather
Salvatore
The Good Society

history. To me, Sicily is the most remarkable land in the entire Italian boot because of its indomitable spirit of survival.

I like to call Sicily the "Hawaii of Italy." Like Hawaii, Sicily is an island separate from the mainland of its mother country. Also like Hawaii, Sicily has a distinct culture, a blend of the numerous cultures that have claimed and occupied the island. Most of all, both the Aloha State and Sicily share a bountiful feeling of hospitality. Sicily and the Sicilians will welcome you with open hearts, eager to share with you the pleasures of their land. As a Sicilian woman, I want to present it to you as something so special that it deserves to be visited over and over again. I guarantee that you will always find things here to do and see and appreciate.

## Palermo

Ladies and gentlemen, this is my hometown! When I think about the city where I spent a great deal of my life, from childhood to a little beyond my teenage years, I really have so much to tell you. Nowhere else have I ever encountered such a rich culture, with treasures all around, and such fun people. Palermo is the capital of Sicily and the fifth largest city in Italy, with almost 1.3 million people.

Palermo is a city with character, and an enduring desire to be recognized for its true history and splendor, and *not* as the land of the Mafia. My job is to introduce you to a city

**TRAVEL TIP** **Think Sicily!** I am puzzled about why so many tourists answer only "Rome, Florence, and Venice" when asked "Where in Italy are you visiting?"—as if no other place could matter. Based on this, I've become a huge ambassador for my own land. And I believe movie director Giuseppe Tornatore feels the same way—he wants to offer a view of Sicily as a land still very much connected to its traditions. I remember his saying, in a conversation I had with him, that Sicily is not about the Mafia; it's about loyalty, family, prosperity, and beauty.

## ON LOCATION SICILY

MOVIE: *Cinema Paradiso*
RELEASE: **1988**
DIRECTOR: **Giuseppe Tornatore**
CAST: **Jacques Perrin, Philippe Noiret,
Marco Leonardi, Salvatore Cascio**

Is there anyone out there who hasn't cried, watching this touching movie? This is for sure one of my favorite movies of all time. As always, Giuseppe Tornatore focuses a lot on the old Sicily, making it so appealing. I am so proud that he and I were born in the same land. He makes Sicilians proud (and the rest of the Italians, too, of course).

It's almost certain that Tornatore injects a bit of his personal life into every single movie he writes or directs. You can sense it in the scenes you watch, the charismatic locations he chooses, and the characters who populate his work. The images in *Cinema Paradiso* remain in your mind, in your heart. They make your spirit soar. This is poetry, music, harmony. They represent pieces of real life and the true values of a society that still follows old traditions.

*Cinema Paradiso is made special by the music composed by Ennio Morricone—according to Tornatore, the only person who could do the job. (I agree, and lucky me to have worked with him!) And did you know that for most of the movies that Maestro Morricone did with Tornatore, he actually wrote the music before the movies were filmed?*

The town in the movie *Cinema Paradiso* (released in Italy as *Nuovo Cinema Paradiso*) is based on **Bagheria**, nine miles east of Palermo (where I come from). Bagheria is where Tornatore was born and raised. And it doesn't really matter to Sicilians if some of the Bagheria portrayed in the movie is fake; in fact, it's Tunisia that we're seeing some of the time.

Tornatore built Giancaldo—his town in *Cinema Paradiso*—as a collage of Sicily. The little town of **Palazzo Adriano**, a main focal point, is situated in the rocky hills in the center of western Sicily, south of Palermo. The 14th-century **Ventimiglia Castle**, which was used as the location for the young hero Salvatore's school, is to the east of Palermo in Castelbuono, near Cefalu.

Palazzo Adriano has a piazza that has changed little over the years. In the movie you see the young Salvatore here by the steps, waiting in the pouring rain for his girl. On the side of the church in the piazza is the wall on which Alfredo projected his first outdoor movie for a piazza full of people.

On the lower floor of the Palazzo Municipale—the town hall—you'll find the Nuovo Cinema Paradiso Museum, with photos taken on the movie set along with props and costumes used by the film's actors. For further exploration, the Museum of the Water has exhibits relating to the town's water sources, rivers, and sea. In the city library, the Museum of the Books displays historic volumes. The museums are open Monday through Sunday from 9 am through 1 pm and 3 to 7 pm.

If you want to follow the footsteps of the movie's stars, I've discovered a unique weekend tour in Palazzo Adriano. The tour is designed mainly for Italians, since it's in Italian with a splash of Sicilian dialect, but you can still enjoy it. Included are Piazza Umberto, the 16th-century Church of Santa Maria Assunta (Greek-Byzantine), the 18th-century Church of Santa Maria del Lume (Latin rites), the Nuevo Cinema Paradiso Museum, Federico Castle (built in 1200), and the Civic Museum of Real Casina (Arberesh culture). • Bookings: Non Solo Pane, phone 3 208 878 863.

*A local specialty served up in the movie is pasta with breadcrumbs, pine nuts, and raisins— accompanied by a steady flow of Sicily's ink-black Nero d'Avola wine.*

*Palermo is one of my favorite places, and not just because it's my home town! It's a beautiful, exciting city with lots to offer.*

that has been ruled by many different civilizations and had many cultures contribute to make it so special. It's a strong city, one that needs to be tasted slowly—like a bottle of great wine.

I have lived in Malibu, California, for a few years now, and I will tell you that Palermo reminds me quite a lot of Southern California. That's not only because of the warm weather (you can visit Palermo at any time of the year, because it's almost always warm). Just like Los Angeles, Palermo is strategically located between the sea and the mountains, the countryside, and arid areas that aren't quite desert but will

remind you a lot of the Palm Springs area.

I grew up spending wintertime in Mondello, the most loved beach area in Palermo, and in the mountains at Piano Battaglia, skiing with my mother. So much fun! But let's get into the core of Palermo with a little history and many unique things that you'll want to see.

This city on the northeast shore of Sicily is almost 3,000 years old! Can you imagine how much history is here? This is a city that has been colonized by many peoples, from the Phoenicians to the Byzantines, the Greeks, the Arabs, and the Normans. And of course one must mention the great Giuseppe Garibaldi, the liberator who united Sicily. The famous general entered

Palermo in 1860 with his troops (the "Thousand"), and the city and all of Sicily became part of the new Kingdom of Italy in 1861.

## Touring the City

There's so much to see in Palermo! Founded in 1143, the glorious **Church of Martorana** is an awesome combination of Byzantine and Norman influence. Seventeenth-century alterations added a baroque flavor. My parents were married here, and I highly recommend it to anyone looking for the most amazing place to marry. It's simply gorgeous. • Piazza Bellini 3, Quattro Canti.

For lovers of the Baroque, another interesting place is

*Giuseppe Garibaldi (1807–1882), the great hero of Italian unification.*

### The Leopard

Sicily was the backdrop for a movie that became a classic for director Luchino Visconti. This is where he shot his 1963 masterpiece *Il Gattopardo—The Leopard*. One of the locations he used was Villa Boscogrande. Also featured were the lovely towns of Ciminna and Cefalu, where the Prince of Salina met the street woman. Ciminna is about 30 miles southeast of Palermo, and Cefalu is on the coast 43 miles east of Palermo.

Palermo

*Cefalu Cathedral is characteristic of the picturesque, Moorish influenced churches of Sicily.*

*The Church of Martorana is a glorious monument to the Norman influence in Sicilian history.*

**Casa Professa (the Church of Jesus, or Chiesa del Gesu)**, built by the Jesuits in the 16th century and later enlarged. The interior is an explosion of ornate stone inlay, wall paintings, and sculpture. Extensive restoration work at the church, bombed during World War II, was completed in 2009. Casa Professa also houses the Municipal Library, containing many early printed works. • Via Casa Professa 21, near Quattro Canti.

The impressive **Palermo Cathedral** dates from 1185 and is a combination of several

*Inside the Casa Professa you'll discover a riot of Baroque splendor.*

*Eclectic and gorgeous, Palermo Cathedral presents a mix of historic architectural styles.*

different architectural styles, thanks to alterations over the centuries. The neoclassical style you see now dates from the 18th century. • Piazza di Cattedrale, Corso Vittorio Emanuele at Via Matteo Bonello.

You'll fall in love with the spectacular **St. John of the Hermits** (known in Italian as Chiesa di San Giovanni degli Eremiti) because of its brilliant red domes, which show the continuing Arab influence in Sicily at the time of its reconstruction in the 12th century. The bell tower, with its arcaded loggias, is instead a typical example of Gothic architecture. • Via dei Benedettini 16, near the Palace of the Normans.

You'll also want to visit **Santa Teresa alla Kalsa** (Church of Santa Teresa), which takes its name from the Arabic *al-khalisa*, meaning "elected." Constructed from 1686 to 1706 over the former emir's residence, the baroque church is filled with beautiful stucco decorations from the early 18th century. • Piazza della Kalsa.

The popular **Palazzo dei Normanni**—Palace of the Normans—is truly one of the most beautiful Italian palaces. Built in the 12th century over an Arab fortress, the palace houses the famous **Palatine Chapel**, lavishly embellished with spectacular Byzantine mosaics. The palace is also the seat of the Sicilian Regional Assembly. • Piazza Indipendenza, Corso Vittorio Emanuele near the Palermo Cathedral.

The Moorish-style **Zisa palace** and less preserved **Cuba** (not the Hispanic one!) were 12th-century summer residences for Palermo's Norman kings, part of a hunting park. Similar buildings were common in northern Africa, but only these remain. The restored Zisa, which houses an Islamic museum, is west of the historic center at Piazza Gugliemo il Buono. Cuba is to the south at Corso Calatafimi (opposite Via Quarta dei Mille). These are wonderful to see but aren't

*The red domes of St. John of the Hermits indicate the historic Arab influence on Sicilian architecture and art.*

*In contrast to the eclecticism of other Sicilian churches, Santa Teresa alla Kalsa has a pure eighteenth century style.*

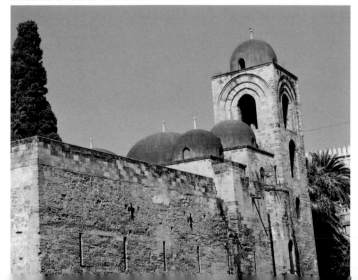

*Once the fortress of the Norman kings, the Palazzo dei Normanni is now the meeting place of the Sicilian Regional Assembly.*

8,000 seats. Since its opening in 1897, singing stars and ballet companies from all over the world have graced this stage. Tenor Enrico Caruso performed during the theater's opening season and returned at the end of his career for *Rigoletto*. And this is where Francis Ford Coppola filmed the dramatic final scenes of *The Godfather: Part III*. • Piazza Giuseppe Verdi, website <u>teatromassimo.it</u>, phone +39 091 6053267; guided tours in English are available Tuesday–Sunday, usually from 9:30 to 4:30.

Another magnificent opera house is **Teatro Politeama**, where the city organizes rare but exciting performances. It was built between 1867 and 1874. • Piazza Ruggero Settimo.

**For shopping**—In Palermo's historical center, **Corso Vittorio Emanuele** and **Via Maqueda** are rich in clothing and shoe stores, home décor and furniture—probably

in the best area of Palermo, so always be cautious with your belongings.

**Regional Archeological Museum Antonio Salinas** is one the premier museums of Italy. Housed in a former monastery, it contains remains from Hellenistic, Roman, and Etruscan civilizations in Italy. • Piazza Olivella 24; open daily.

In the middle of the city, the **Teatro Massimo** is one of the most prestigious opera houses in all of Italy. It is with great pride that I tell you that this is the largest theater in Italy and the third largest in Europe, with

*Built by Arab craftsmen for the Norman king of Sicily, the Zisa is full of Moorish-style details.*

*Part of the collection of ancient art in the Regional Archeological Museum Antonio Salinas.*

*The Teatro Massimo in Palermo is the largest opera house in all of Italy.*

the best deals that you'll find in the entire city. Still in the old town center, head off of Via Maqueda (which merges with via Roma Vecchia) across the **Piazza della Vergogna** or Square of the Embarrassed Statues—called this because the sculpted figures of the 16th-century fountain are all naked. Running to the right and left is **Vicoli di Sant'Agostino**, where street markets are open all day long to sell everything from clothing to shoes to art—at a very low cost.

You will also find lots of knockoffs of Valentino, Versace, Gucci; these are all fake purses, belts, and sunglasses. Be aware that the police are very vigilant, and you could be fined or even arrested if caught buying these illegal fake brands. Make sure that what you buy is legitimate, and always get a receipt.

*The Teatro Politeama, not as large or presigious as the Teatro Massimo, but perhaps more beautiful.*

## Mondello

Now we are in one of my favorite places in the entire universe. When I was a child my mother used to bring me to Mondello, only a 20-minute ride from Palermo by way of Parco della Favorita. The Parco della Favorita is a long, green boulevard that belonged to the aristocracy in the late 1800s; in modern times it lost a bit of its charm, but it's still the fastest way to get to Mondello.

Mondello is more than just a beach resort: it's a way of life for Palermitans, a Sicilian ritual. It's the perfect mix of familiarity and beauty, where families, friends, and tourists

*The Piazza della Vergogna, or Square of the Embarrassed Statues. I don't know—they don't look that embarrassed to me.*

Mondello's summer season runs from May to September, but the weather is so warm that you could stretch it through November. Every summer, Mondello is the setting for the Windsurf World Festival, when surfers from all over the world come to compete. I covered it a few years ago when I had my own show on Italian television, and it is quite a spectacle of cultures and excitement.

Tourists from all over the world come to Mondello, so sometimes in the summer the crowds make it almost impossible to visit—and to park, if you're driving. You'll find cars parked up on the curbs and in areas where they aren't supposed to be at all. If you follow this example, though, you'll be fined and, even worse, may not be able

celebrate the white and golden beach and turquoise sea. There are pedal-boats for hire, lifeguards keeping an eye on the water, and vendors offering iced coconuts and ice cream. Mondello has fun little shops built on the beach as well as beautiful Italian villas—reminiscent of an Italian version of Miami's South Beach. Street vendors are here to try to sell you all sorts of fashionable hats and dresses as well as tasty delicacies found nowhere else.

There are three ways to enjoy the beach at Mondello, depending on how much you want to pay. For a small fortune (over $500 per month), you can rent a little cabin all to yourself. For a modest amount of money, you can enjoy *lidi attrezzati*, summer beach establishments with chairs, umbrellas, and other perks. The open sand between the cabins, the *lidi*, and the sea are free—but you'd better arrive early in the day to claim a spot!

### Sounds a Little Fishy!

The popular fish market in the heart of Palermo is known as the **Vucciria**, which means "confusion" in Sicilian. Don't ask me why—perhaps because during the early part of the day the market is filled with people.
• Piazza San Domenica; open Monday–Saturday from early morning to early afternoon.

*A typical street vendor of the Vucciria.*

to find your car! (But that isn't going to stop the Palermitans.)

The public transportation is very useful, or you can just book a hotel and stay right in town.

**Getting to Mondello—** Mondello is on Palermo's urban bus network, and standard tickets for the AMAT city buses (including good-value day tickets) are valid as far as Mondello, making it a cheap and easy outing from central Palermo. Buses 806 and 833 run to Mondello from the Politeama and Piazza Sturzo in Palermo. In summer there is also another line (GT or Gran Turismo) operating more comfortable coaches; details can be found on the AMAT city bus website (amat.pa.it) along with details of the regular urban routes.

## Santa Lucia, Too

Santa Lucia, the patron saint of Syracuse, is another saint beloved by Sicilians. During her feast day on December 13, people don't eat anything made with flour but instead boil wheat in its natural state and use it to prepare a special meal called *cuccia* (pronounced "coo-chee-

*The former Charleston Restaurant, featured in* The Sicilian.

### Mondello in the Movies

One of the most unforgettable eateries in Mondello was a setting for American director Michael Cimino's 1987 film *The Sicilian*, with Christopher Lambert. The Charleston Restaurant, right on the beach, opened in 1913 and was a favorite of politicians and royalty; it has since changed hands.

*A statue of Santa Lucia, carried in a procession on her feast day, December 13.*

*Mondello, a beautiful resort town on clear Mediterranean waters.*

aw"). St. Lucia is believed to have saved the city of Syracuse from starvation in 1582 when a ship full of grain mysteriously arrived in port. People were so hungry that they didn't wait to make flour for bread, instead eating the grain as it had arrived.

## Getting to and around Palermo

Palermo is an important link among the cities of Sicily and a key node in the Sicilian road network. It's the junction of the A19 highway east to Trapani, the A29 southwest to the international airport, the A19 southwest to Messina, and the A20 to Catania. Palermo is one of the main cities on the trans-European route E90.

**Traveling by air**—Palermo International Airport is 20 miles west of the city at Punta Raisi. Also known as Falcone-Borsellino or Punta Raisi, the

**TRAVEL TIP** To find out more about all things Palermo, visit palermo-sicilia.it/english

*A vista of the Aranella in Palermo.*

## Local Flavor

The food is fantastic in Mondello! Try the *panellas* and *crocchè* (little chickpea cakes and fried potato cakes), as well as the Palermitan *astigliola*—something that might not be appealing to many of you, as it consists of pig intestines, grilled and flavored with lemon and spices. I know that doesn't sound good, but it really is. I recall being with my mother as a child on our little Vespa and stopping for astigliola right at the end of Favorita Boulevard. (Yes, my mother has always ridden motorcycles, and I would go with her all the time as a child.) Street vendors will sell you some for a dollar.

We eat *pasta al forno* in small local restaurants (similar to baked mostaccioli but made with little pasta rings), and also *arancinas*, scrumptious fried rice balls containing meat or cheese, just delicious. No one can beat Sicilian cuisine!

The best *pasta allo scoglio* you can have is also prepared in Mondello. There are many variations of this classic pasta with seafood, but they all start with clams and mussels. Here's how you can recreate the flavor of Mondello at home:

### Pasta allo Scoglio

Here's an overview of how to prepare a fresh, delicious tasting dish: Wash fresh clams and let them soak in salted water for at least two hours to eliminate residual sand. Drain the clams. Heat olive oil in a large skillet over low heat; add some minced garlic to the pan along with chiles (as per your taste) and cook until the garlic is lightly colored. Pour in a glass of white wine and the clams (and maybe mussels, too) and let it all cook together for a few minutes. Keep everything on low heat and stir occasionally. Now, cut the tomatoes in half, pour them into the pan, and mix them thoroughly with the seafood.

Meanwhile, cook the pasta. Then drain and add the pasta to the skillet. Let it all jumble together for a few seconds so the noodles take on the taste of the shellfish. Sprinkle on a bit of chopped parsley and serve piping hot. *Buon divertimento!*

## Palermo's Patron Saint

Palermitans are mainly Catholics, and their love for their saints is a cultural priority. In fact, the July 15 celebration of the city's patron saint, Santa Rosalia, is the most important event of the year besides Christmas.

Tradition says that when Santa Rosalia's relics were carried around the city three times in 1624, the plague was lifted from the city. My own mother told me that when I was a little girl, I was about to lose my sight and so she prayed to Santa Rosalia. My eyesight was saved! I am a huge believer, and I think that Santa Rosalia must still watch over me.

The saint's remains are protected in the Sanctuary of Santa Rosalia at the top of Mount Pellegrino, overlooking the sea north of the city. A small chapel built into the hill contains a statue of the saint and a glass coffin where believers have deposited jewels and money in thanks for graces received.

Not only is it wonderful to see all of this, but at the bakery next to the sanctuary you can taste a delicious baked ricotta cake that you won't find anyplace else in the world. You have to try it!

You can reach the sanctuary on a wonderfully panoramic bus ride. From the main train station in Palermo, take bus 139e to Via Monte Pellegrino (you're not there yet, despite the name), and from there take bus 812 to the sanctuary. The ride takes about 45 minutes. • Santuario Santa Rosalia, Opera Don Orione, Via Pietro Bonanno, Monte Pellegrino, phone +39 091 540326; open daily.

*The sanctuary of Santa Rosalia is carved directly into the rock of a hill.*

 **More Sun and Sand**

Another lovely seaside area is the Arenella in Palermo—maybe a bit rockier than Mondello, but with sandy white beaches. The water is clearer and cleaner to swim in here, but you do need to wear plastic water shoes to walk through the rocks. It's beautiful, though!

airport is dedicated to Giovanni Falcone and Paolo Borsellino, two anti-Mafia judges who were killed by the Mafia in the early 1990s.

Palermo-Boccadifalco Airport is the city's second airport, offering noncommericial and charter flights.

**Traveling by rail**—The main rail station is Palermo Centrale. Frequent trains connect the Centrale, Notarbartolo, and Francia stations with the international airport. You can access cities throughout Sicily by train from Palermo; visit trenitalia.com to check schedules.

**Traveling by bus**—The Palermo public bus system is operated by AMAT, with 90 lines reaching every part of the city. AST buses connect Palermo to other cities in Sicily. More information is available at AMAT's website, amat.pa.it.

**Traveling by sea**—The port of Palermo was founded more than 2,700 years ago and is the main gateway to Sicily, along with the port of Messina. From here, ferries link Palermo with the mainland as well as islands such as Ustica and the Aeolians (in summer via Cefalù). This is also an important port for cruise ships.

**Traveling by car**—Avis has offices all over Sicily. Be super careful as you drive the intricate roads and streets of

> "Who goes out of the house makes it!" Sicilians mean that if you get yourself out there in the world, you will make it!

Italy, especially in Sicily and Palermo. People even drive over the curbs—there isn't much order, unfortunately. Stay alert, or you could end up in an accident. Also make sure to lock your car, and don't stop for any reason on the street or highway. I don't mean to make you paranoid, but while Italians are very friendly, you just never know, no matter where you travel. I'm sure you don't pick up hitchhikers in your own city, right?

## The Aeolian Islands

Off its northern shore, Sicily has its own island escapes. The Aeolian Islands are popular for their gorgeous scenery, beaches, and thermal resorts, and they've been used as settings for a number of films. **Salina Island** was one of the locations for *Il Postino* (see page 97).

Largest of the islands is **Lipari**, with a castle complex that shows evidence of Greek, Spanish, and Norman days. In fact, the island has been inhabited since the 5th

century BC. The **Eoliano Archaeological Museum** here is excellent.

**Vulcano Island** is loved by tourists from all over the world—because of its mud! (Don't let the island's name throw you; this is very much an inactive volcano.) You'll wonder why this stinky mud should be such an appealing thing, but Its health properties are said to be incredible. Doctors recommend

### Romina's Hotel Picks

**CAPOFARO MALVASIA & RESORT**
*Via Faro 3*
*98050 Salina*
***Website:*** *capofaro.it*
***Phone:*** *+39 090 9844330*

**HOTEL PRINCIPE DI RINELLA**
*Via S. Gaetano Leni*
*98050 Salina*
***Website:***
  *hotelprincipedisalina.it*
***Phone:*** *+39 090 9809308*

*The castle of Lipari.*

that patients come here and immerse themselves in the strong-smelling stuff! Whether you have rheumatic pain or a wound or just skin impurities, Vulcano is something you should experience. (A disclaimer here: I'm a singer, not a doctor, and I'm only reporting what people have told me. I cannot guarantee how you'll feel afterward.)

The islands can be reached by ferry or hydrofoil from Milazzo, Messina, Palermo, and Naples. For details, visit: www.thethinkingtraveller.com/thinksicily.

*Movie Trivia*

*Director Roberto Rossellini fell in love with actress Ingrid Bergman as he was filming his 1950 movie* Terra di Dio *on Stromboli in the Aeolian Islands.*

## Messina

The city of Messina is just across from the toe of Italy's boot—in fact, the Strait of Messina is less than 2 miles wide at its narrowest point. Besides being a gateway to Sicily and a hub for travel to other island cities, Messina has been a frequent filming location. Scenes in

*Malèna, The Godfather II,* and *Il Postino* were shot here.

From Messina, it's just 36 miles west to the **Sanctuary of the Black Madonna of Tindari**. On a rocky hill

## ON LOCATION SICILY

MOVIE: *Il Postino (The Postman)*
RELEASE: **1994**
DIRECTOR: **Michael Radford**
CAST: **Massimo Troisi, Maria Grazia Cucinotta, Philippe Noiret**

*Il Postino* is a 1994 movie directed by Michael Radford and written by its star, Massimo Troisi. Massimo postponed heart surgery to complete this beautiful movie; he died a day after the filming was finished. Troisi was one of Italy's most loved actors, and he will never be forgotten.

The film tells a fictional story in which the real-life poet Pablo Neruda (Philippe Noiret)

*Il Postino was made for $3 million and grossed more than $75 million. The movie was so successful that it ran in New York theaters for more than two years.*

forms a wonderful friendship with a postman (Troisi) who loves poetry. The postman falls in love with Beatrice, played by Maria Grazia Cucinotta. Some scenes in *Il Postino* were shot on the Neapolitan island of Procida (see page 76). The other beach shown

in the movie and the house in which Neruda lived are on the Aeolian island of **Salina** about 50 miles north of Sicily. The house is a private residence in the village of Pollara. Unfortunately, I've heard that the beach has been terribly damaged by people who have dumped garbage, taken away pebbles, and disrespected nature. Please do care about the beaches; it is our job, for the future of our children.

*Massimo Troisi was so weak during the filming that all his scenes were done in just two takes. A lookalike stand-in ended up doing the longer sequences— including the scenes where he's riding a bicycle.*

Salina is about a 1 1/2-hour trip from Milazzo.

*The musical score by Luis Enriquez Bacalov won the Academy Award for best music (original dramatic score). The movie received four other Oscar nominations as well, including one for best picture.*

above the Tyrrhenian Sea, the sanctuary stands on the site of the ancient Greek town of Tindaris. Legend has it that the statue was brought here sometime in the latter half of the first milleniium when the ship carrying it was forced ashore by a storm.

Messina is connected to the mainland by ferry and hydrofoil; it's about 20 minutes by ferry to Villa San Giovanni or by hydrofoil to Reggio di Calabria, site of the closest airport. You can also come by train; the cars cross the strait on barges. Train and bus services link Messina with cities throughout Sicily. (Here's a link for more information: tripadvisor.com/Travel-g187889-s301/Messina.)

*The famous Black Madonna of Tindari.*

## Interview with Director Gian Paolo Cugno

**Gian Paolo Cugno** directed the 2006 movie *Salvatore*—the only film produced by Disney in Italy—and the 2010 movie *The Good Society (La Bella Società)*. Both were filmed in Sicily. I spoke with him about the two films, his directing, and the island of Sicily.

**Q: Can you tell us where the idea for *Salvatore* came from and how you chose the locations at which to shoot it?**

**A:** I decided to make this movie when I discovered the true story of a little boy who loses his parents and has to face life on his own, at a young age, with trials and tribulations. This happened in the little village where I was born and where I shot the movie, Pachino, in the province of Syracuse, right on the sea.

**Q: Can you tell us what made you choose the locations?**

**A:** The movie was shot in the same place where the true story occurred. There is a location on the beach, right across the sea from Africa, where the shores are so white and the rocks are white and the beaches are wide and not typically Sicilian. That gave a poetic accent to the atmosphere of my movie (something that the American people should come and enjoy and discover), making our set naturally beautiful. This is exactly what Disney and I were looking for!

*The splendid town hall of Noto.*

*Piazza Duomo in Syracuse.*

**TRAVEL TIP** Domestic flights between cities in Italy can be extremely cheap, especially if you book them weeks in advance. Sometimes you can fly from Rome to Sicily for only $30! Of course, I have to give a disclaimer here, as this doesn't happen all the time—only at certain times of the year, or if you book far ahead—and every airline's fees are subject to change.

## ON LOCATION SICILY

MOVIE: *Malèna*
RELEASE: 2000
DIRECTOR: **Giuseppe Tornatore**
CAST: **Monica Bellucci, Giuseppe Suilfaro, Luciano Federico**

My dear *paisano* Giuseppe Tornatore came back to Sicily to shoot *Malèna*, starring the breathtaking model-actress Monica Bellucci. The movie takes place in the 1940s during World War II, telling the story of a beautiful woman whose husband dies in the war. She is suddenly desired by every man in her small village, making the other women extremely jealous—to the point of brutally punishing Malèna for her beauty and for seducing their men, through no fault of her own.

I recorded a song from *Malèna* in the track titled "Solo Noi" for my album with composer Ennio Morricone titled *Morricone Uncovered*, with lyrics that I wrote at the request of the maestro. If you like this movie, you'll love the soundtrack.

The most important scenes of *Malèna* were shot in the beautiful little village of **Noto**— though in the movie it's called Castelcuto. Situated southwest of Syracuse near Sicily's southern tip, Noto is known for its baroque style and 18th-century buildings, and also for its fine wines. It has been declared a World Heritage Site by UNESCO.

In the marvelous city of **Syracuse** (Siracusa), you can see the square where the men stare as Malèna (Monica Belluci) walks around, and the women decide to attack her. The square is called **Piazza Duomo**, and it's in the old part of the city on Ortigia island. Ortigia is just off the promenade called Passeggio Aretusa, not far from the Fountain of Aretusa. You won't have any problem finding it—there are signs everywhere. In Piazza Duomo, you will find the Cathedral of Santa Lucia built over the remains of a Greek temple, the Temple of Athena—something you don't want to miss.

Other filming was done 75 miles north of Syracuse at **Taormina**—another of my favorite places in the world! The drive along the island's east coast takes about 1 1/2 hours. A number of scenes in *Malèna* took place in Taormina's luxurious San Domenico Palace Hotel. Check it out and live in the beautiful atmosphere of Taormina!

Additional scenes were shot across the island at the white cliffs of **Scala dei Turchi** (on the southwest coast near Agrigento) and among ruins left after a 1968 earthquake destroyed the town of **Poggioreale**. (The town was rebuilt nearby.)

**Q: What do you like the most about your city? And about Sicily?**
**A:** What I love about my city is a special light that comes through, especially in wintertime. It's hard to describe, but it's the perfect lighting when it comes to shooting a movie. Just like in New Zealand, in Sicily you have the beauty to shoot any genre of movie outdoors.

**Q: What would you like for the American and world audience to know about Sicily? What is your vision?**
**A:** I would love for Americans and the rest of the world not to focus so much on the Mafia. At the end of the day, that is really everywhere, criminality is everywhere. Instead I'd love for people, maybe through my movies, to find out how welcoming are the places and how hospitable are our inhabitants, as well as finding out how sweet it can be to live

*Bar Vitelli, a quiet place made internationally famous by* The Godfather.

## ON LOCATION SICILY

MOVIE: *The Godfather*
RELEASE: 1972
DIRECTOR: Francis Ford Coppola
CAST: Marlon Brando, Al Pacino, James Caan

In *The Godfather*, Michael Corleone (Al Pacino) flees to Sicily after murdering the gangster Virgil Sollozzo (Al Lettiere) and his henchman, the corrupt police captain Mark McCluskey (Sterling Hayden).

All the Sicily scenes in *The Godfather* were actually filmed in Sicily. Studio executives had wanted the film to be filmed on their back lot to save money, but Coppola insisted on authentic location shooting, so there are lots of fun *Godfather* locations to see in Sicily!

Our first stop is the famous **Bar Vitelli**, where Michael Corleone met his beautiful but doomed Sicilian wife Apollonia (Simonetta Stefanelli). Bar Vitelli is still open for business in the village of **Savoca**, 18 miles southwest of Messina (near Taormina). Savoca was a stand-in for the town of Corleone in the movie.

Also in Savoca is the church where Michael marries Apollonia, the **Chiesa di Santa Lucia**. Later Apollonia dies in a car bombing intended for Michael outside their Sicilian home, which is actually the **Castello degli Schiavi** in Fiumefreddo, a few miles south of Taormina. Other "Corleone" scenes were shot in the medieval town of **Forza d'Agro**, near Taormina and the Mount Etna volcano.

The real **Corleone** is a more developed town about 35 miles south of Palermo. This is a place with a strong history of families who have worked hard and fought to protect their lands. That is the essential truth about Corleone, though there are many stories that people talk about; I will let others form their own opinions. You can contact the mayor's office at the Corleone City Hall to find out more about the town, but I warn you that most likely they won't be able to speak English!
• Piazza Garibaldi 1, 90034 Corleone; phone +39 091 8467577.

*Italian actor Raoul Bova (left) talks with director Gian Paolo Cugno on the set of* The Good Society (La Bella Societé). *Raul is also the love interest of Diane Lane in* Under the Tuscan Sun *(page 133). I've met Raul, and he's fantastic (and, if I may say so, gorgeous).* PHOTO: PARRINELLO

direct my first big movie in my own land, with hugely famous actors like Giancarlo Giannini and Enrico Lo Verso, working on a true story, with a screenplay entirely written by me—it has been truly exciting and empowering.

As far as The Good Society, the movie was shot in the center of Sicily in the city of Enna, between the immense gold fields of corn and the little villages that still have a medieval look, it was just perfect for a film that embraces a length of time from the 60s through the 80s.

in Sicily, being kissed every day by the sunshine, throughout the year!

**Q: Both of your movies have been shot in Sicily and received huge acclaim. Can you please tell us more?**
**A:** *Salvatore* was the first Disney product done in Italy and distributed by Buena Vista International. It has been a magnificent experience. To

**Q: Critics in America have called you the new Tornatore; how does this make you feel? If you could base your next movie in Sicily, where would you film it?**

## Romina's Hotel Picks

**SAN DOMENICO PALACE HOTEL**
*Piazza San Domenico 5*
*98039 Taormina*
**Website:** san-domenico-palace.com
**Phone:** +39 0942 613111

**LA PLAGE RESORT**
*Isola Bella, Via Nazionale 107/A*
*98039 Taormina*
**Website:** laplageresort.com
**Phone:** +39 0942 626095

*The ruins of the Greek theater are one of the notable historic sights in the ancient city of Taormina.*

*The Scala dei Turchi ("Stairs of the Turks"), the white cliffs on the southwest coast of Sicily.*

**A:** I prefer that my filmmaking be recognized as a labor of love by a young Italian filmmaker with an international flavor. I sincerely love my Italianship and my Sicilianship, but I also feel very much projected—I believe this is a perfect word for me, one who projects for a living!—outside the Italian territory. As a matter of fact, my next film will be in China, based on a beautiful Chinese tale. However, my biggest dream is Hollywood, and I think that eventually my work will be more and more appreciated there, bringing the best of Italy to all with wonderful stories that I am sure the American public will love.

I am ready to direct!

## Interview with Actor Enrico Lo Verso

**Enrico Lo Verso** starred in both *Salvatore* and *The Good Society*. He is also known in the U.S. for his starring role in the 1994 musical movie *Farinelli*. I asked the actor about his work in the two made-in-Sicily movies.

**Q: What is your favorite scene in the film *The Good Society*?**
**A:** I like the scene of the barricade—an incredible and epic scene where I express, before I die, the true nature of the young main character who wants to live at all costs, in the center of the protest, to feel alive at this moment of his existence.

**Q: What do you like the most about the location where *Salvatore* was filmed?**
**A:** In the movie *Salvatore* (subtitled *This Is Life*), I love the scene filmed among the rocks where Salvatore fixes the boat engine and for the first time trusts me as his maestro (his master or mentor, for lack of a better word), asking me for help to accomplish his task.

The location where Salvatore lives is on the beach, in the extreme south of Italy and, of course, Sicily, a place truly magical that has an exotic African accent.

**Q: Give me three words to describe Sicily.**
**A:** Let me just tell you this: Sicily is a beautiful disease that no one can ever heal from.

**Q: Tell me about your experience working with director Gian Paolo Cugno.**
**A:** Gian Paolo Cugno is a director with great vision, great tales, incredibly disciplined, and a perfectionist. He is definitely ready to make the biggest jump of his career, with larger international productions, supercharged by his incredible passion!

## Interview with Actor Giancarlo Giannini

**Giancarlo Giannini** starred in Gian Paolo Cugno's *The Good Society*, but American audiences may be more likely to remember him as one of the stars of the beautiful romantic American movie from 1995 filmed with Anthony Quinn and Keanu Reeves titled *A Walk in the Clouds*. He also starred in the blockbuster *Hannibal*, starring Anthony Hopkins, which was filmed in Italy.

*Mt. Etna in one of its more tranquil moods, covered with snow. The city of Catania is in the foreground.*

**Q. Tell us of your experience on the set of *The Good Society*.**

**A.** Gian Paolo is passionate and poetic. Everything he does on set gratifies me as an actor, allowing me to express myself to the fullest but without ever moving too far away from the role. And of course Sicily is an extraordinary island, rich in history and character, and, like a beautiful woman, is meant to explore and enjoy to the fullest.

**Q. Was there a particular location you most appreciated?**

**A.** The Sicilian hinterland is a unique and beautiful landscape—quite magnificent. I remember the endless, rolling hills planted with wheat, which give the island a sense of infinite peace.

### Did You Know?

Director George Lucas used footage of Mount Etna's 2002 eruption to help out with special effects in his 2005 movie *Star Wars Episode III: Revenge of the Sith*. Pretty cool! Many celebrities have chosen to live in the region of the volcano in eastern Sicily, despite the always-present possibility of an eruption. Mick Hucknell, the lead singer of the band Simply Red, not only lives nearby, but he has a very successful winery, which produces wine under the label *Il Cantante* (The Singer). Incredible but true, the ashes of Etna help vineyards to grow strong and the grapes to taste delicious.

**Q. *Hannibal* was filmed in Florence. What do you think of the city?**

**A.** OK. First thing first. Working with a great director like Ridley Scott and a good colleague like Anthony Hopkins was really interesting and powerful. As for Florence, the art and civilization of the place, and its history during the Renaissance, make it a city without equal.

# 10

# The Ancient World of Venice

*"I love to travel, but hate to arrive."* —ALBERT EINSTEIN

*Approaching the island of Venice from the Grand Canal, with a view of the Biblioteca Nazionale Marciana, the Doge's Palace, and St. Mark's Campanile.*

## VENICE

Venezia or Venice—no matter what you call it, this city will seduce you and take you in. Venice is one of those dreamlike places that filmmakers cannot live without. Movies such as *The Merchant of Venice, Dangerous Beauty, The Talented Mr. Ripley,* and *Don't Look Now* have left incredible memories in our hearts. Their stories are rich and passionate, full of intricacies and desperation and drama—the perfect companion to Italy!

This historic city on Italy's northeast coast is actually a conglomerate of 100 islands connected by 400 bridges. Everything here is boats—from romantic gondolas and water taxis to garbage boats, ambulance boats, and police boats. That's the main reason Venice is so expensive: everything has to be brought by boat and hand-trucked to its destination.

You must be prepared to do lots of walking in Venice,

because if suddenly you want to return to your hotel, there's no other option but to walk back—or swim! My suggestion is to let your heart lead the way when it comes to strolling around and discovering the city. You might find yourself in front of a stunning church or amazing monument you wouldn't encounter on an organized tour.

## Seeing the City

Let's get right into the heart of the lagoon city the Italians call La Serenissima—"the very serene city." Piazza San Marco—**St. Mark's Square**—is the city's main square, and one of the most amazing places to visit in Venice. It's a mélange of ancient styles, including Byzantine and Islamic elements. Important scenes in many movies have taken place here—*The Tourist*, *The Talented Mr. Ripley*, and *Indiana Jones and the Last Crusade*, to mention just a few.

The magnificent **St. Mark's Basilica** was consecrated in 1094. Its interior is covered in millions and millions of tiny glass pieces the size of your pinky nail, everything sandwiched between gold. More magnificent mosaics can be seen in the lunettes (the half-

An aerial view of the Venetian Lagoon, looking to the southwest.

moon spaces above the arches). That is why it is a great idea to visit in the early part of the day when the sun is up, so you see them at their most glorious!
• Website www.basilicasanmarco.it, phone (tours) +39 041 241 3817; guided tours available April–October, daily except Sunday.

The **Doge's Palace** is another beautiful Venetian trademark on the square. The elegant Gothic palace, begun around 1340 and rebuilt over the centuries after several fires, was both the residence of Venice's top authority and the seat of the government. Now it houses the **Museo dell'Op-**

Entering St. Mark's Square, with the Doge's Palace on the right and St. Mark's Basilica ahead.

**era** on the ground floor, displaying decorations from the original façade. You can take a special tour to see the Doge's opulent apartments upstairs, the government council chambers, the armory—and some prisons. You *must* make your reservation in advance, as there

*Some of the magnificent mosaics inlaid in gold inside St. Mark's. This is why St. Marks is called La Chiesa d'Oro, or The Church of Gold.*

*A detail of the entrance to St. Mark's Basilica. The horses on the balcony were looted from the Hippodrome of Constantinople during the Fourth Crusade in 1204.*

*St. Mark's Basilica, one of the greatest glories of Venice and an enduring symbol of the city.*

*The Doge's Palace. It's a beautiful museum now, but once upon a time it was the residence of one of the most powerful men in Europe.*

*A glass maker in Murano, where the finest glass of the Renaissance was made.*

are only a few organized tours throughout the week. A single ticket gives you admission to the Doge's palace and other museums on the square, including **Museo Correr** (art and history) and **Museo Archeo-logico Nazionale**. • Palazzo Ducale, San Marco 1, 30135 Venice, palazzoducale.visit-muve.it, phone (bookings) +39 041 42730892.

When it comes to the arts, Venice is also the queen of an enchanting palace that houses the **Peggy Guggenheim Collection** of 20th-century art. You can find yourself moved to tears as you view a memorable Picasso, Dali, or Pollock—just stunning. The building itself—the Palazzo Venier dei Leoni—was begun in the mid-18th century but never finished; Peggy Guggenheim bought it in 1949 and lived here for 30 years. It's on the Grand Canal between the Church of Santa Maria della Salute and the Accademia Bridge. • 704 Dorsoduro, website www. guggenheim-venice.it, phone +39 041 2405411; open daily

(except Tuesday) from 10 am to 6 pm.

As an international popera artist, I naturally want you to know about one of the most exquisite opera houses in the world: **La Fenice**. For more than 200 years, this theater has hosted the greatest singers in the world. It has also been seen in several movies, including

1997's *The Fifth Element*, directed by Luc Besson, in which a strange opera singer—half woman, half alien—hypnotizes the audience with her incredible voice. La Fenice means "the Phoenix," because the theater has risen from the ashes several times since the original building burned in 1774. In the late 90s a terrible fire again destroyed

**TRAVEL TIP** When you get to San Marco Square or any other major Italian area, you may be stopped by people carrying roses. (Most likely they won't be Italians.) They will try to sell you a rose, and you'll probably decline, so then they will tell you that they are tired and you can have all the roses for free! What a wonderful thing; there you are with the love of your life, listening to the music of the heart (Romina Arena, perhaps?), walking through the most romantic city on earth with a bouquet of roses. Well, most likely you will tell the person who handed you the roses that you don't want to take advantage of him. He'll keep telling you that it is a gift, so you'll feel indebted and open your wallet, and perhaps you'll have a 20- or 50-euro note but no change. You'll ask if he has change. Of course, he says, but the moment he takes your money—well, you can say goodbye to your euros, as it will take very fast legs to go after him through the crowded square. You might want to keep a euro or two on the side, just for little emergencies like this! And never open your wallet in a public place for anyone to see. Just say no and walk on.

The home of the Peggy Guggenhem Collection, one of the world's greatest collections of modern art.

Brightly colored houses are a tradition of Burano.

it. After years of rebuilding, the magnificent structure reopened in 2003. It is worth trying to catch a show or at least taking a tour inside, including the delightful dressing rooms and some unique memorabilia of the great soprano and diva extraordinaire Maria Callas. You can get to La Fenice from San Marco Square by taking the vaporetto water bus and stopping at Santa Maria Del Giglio. • Campo San Fantine 1965, website www. teatrolafenice.it, phone +39 041 786511.

Among the other things you'll want to see are the islands of **Murano** and **Burano** in the lagoon a mile to the north. Murano is famous for its blown glass (they do amazingly delicate home décor pieces), and Burano is known for its lace-making and its cheerfully colored houses.

To view frescos by the legendary artist Giotto that almost seem to be created in 3D, you must visit the **Scrovegni Chapel** in the nearby city of **Padua**! Reservations are required; you can prepay by going to www. cappelladegliscrovegni.it, a useful website that also gives

The splendid interior of La Fenice is actually a modern recreation of the nineteenth century interior, which had been gutted by a blaze in 1996. True to its name, La Fenice has several times been destroyed by fire.

**TRAVEL TIP** The best time to visit Venice is between May and September. It's very expensive then, but worth it! After September the rainy season kicks in, and the shops and hotels in Venice have to deal with water problems. Many shops will offer to help you stay dry by selling boots.

Of course, you can visit in February for the annual Carnival (see page 104), when San Marco Square takes on a thousand different colors. But be prepared to encounter showers and chilly weather.

other tips about Venice, Padua, and nearby attractions. • Piazza Eremitani 8, Padua, phone +39 049 2010020; open Monday–Friday from 9 am to 7 pm, Saturday to 6 pm.

**TRAVEL TIP** When you walk into a bar, check the wall. There should be a little poster—the *listino prezzi*—that shows the prices for all the food and beverages. What we call bars in Italy function as places where you can stand and drink or eat something quickly, unless there are also tables outside. But don't buy something at the bar and try to take it to a table—the waiters will yell at you!

*The kiss of Judas, a detail from Scrovegni Chapel's fine frescos by Giotto.*

## Coffee Culture

In Venice—actually, anywhere in Italy—there is something called "the culture of the coffee." What this means is that the moment you sit down at your own table and chair in a square (such as the Piazza San Marco or Piazza di Spagna), you're paying for a piece of real estate. While you can sip a glass of wine standing at a bar for maybe €4 to €7, when you are seated, don't have a panic attack if your bill says €20.

And that delicious espresso that might be 80 cents, standing at the bar? You can expect it to cost a bit over €5! If a small ensemble plays romantic music while you are enjoying your expensive coffee, expect to pay about €15 for that 80-cent coffee. I'm not kidding! The best thing you can do is to keep walking and rest your feet at one of the many benches you'll find throughout the city. Or you can just decide to enjoy the good life and indulge in the perks that money can buy. Grab your travel journal or some postcards, enjoy your coffee and a delicious Italian pastry, and take the time to write about your adventures.

*The sidewalk café is one of the great luxuries of Italy, but luxury has its price.*

## Venice All Year Long

Let's take a look at some of the unique events that take place throughout the year in this city.

**Regata delle Befane.** On January 6, five veteran gondoliers (55 or older) in traditional Epiphany costumes compete on the Grand Canal aboard single-oar *mascareta*

boats. The brief but intense race runs from San Tomà to Rialto.

**Carnevale (Carnival).** For two weeks (usually in February), parades and masquerade balls, traditional ceremonies, concerts, theatrical shows, and general gaiety enliven every square and alley of the city. Many little shops sell wonderful masks to bring home with you. Carnevale ends with Shrove Tuesday, 40 days before Easter. Details: carnevale.venezia.it.

**Festa della Sensa**. Venice celebrates its "Wedding with the Sea" on the weekend following Ascension Day (40 days after Easter). In this ceremony, more than a thousand years old, the Doge (now represented by the Mayor of Venice) is paraded on the *bucentaur* (state barge) in front of the church of San Nicolò

*The world-famous Ponte di Rialto. Building a stone bridge over the Grand Canal was considered risky; an architectural expert predicted the bridge would collapse. But the bridge has been standing since 1591.*

**TRAVEL TIP**

### No Sunbathing, Please

You can't just stop on a bridge and decided to sunbathe or have a picnic! The police patrol the bridges, and if you're caught in the act, they will even give you an expensive ticket. Avoid any of this and move on to a nearby area or a café.

## ON LOCATION VENICE

MOVIE: *The Merchant of Venice*
RELEASE: **2004**
DIRECTOR: **Michael Radford**
CAST: **Al Pacino, Joseph Fiennes, Jeremy Irons**

I have great personal affection and respect for actor Al Pacino, as I was very close to his father Sal, and I've loved all of his roles over the years. But his work in this film version of Shakespeare's *The Merchant of Venice* really took my breath away.

The film opens with images of Venetian life in 1596, especially discrimination against the Jews. Words on the screen inform the audience about anti-Semitism during this period. Shylock (Al Pacino) and Antonio (Jeremy Irons) are seen in a crowd of people watching Jews being thrown into the Grand Canal from the **Rialto**

**Bridge**. Still a main city thoroughfare, the Rialto is the oldest of the four bridges crossing the canal. The iconic stone arch was finished in 1591.

Among other Venice filming locations for the movie, a section of the **Doge's Palace** was used for the scene where Shylock says, "I shall have my bond."

---

*The prostitutes in* The Merchant of Venice *are shown with bared breasts for the sake of historical accuracy. The authorities of the time were disturbed by widespread homosexuality in the city, so by Venetian law all prostitutes had to dress as women and display their female attributes.*

at the Lido, and a gold ring is tossed into the water.

**Vogalonga.** One day every May, this rowing marathon winds along 30 kilometers (18 miles) of the lagoon, attracting aficionados from all over the world. The starting point is in front of the Doge's Palace.

**Festival of the Redeemer.** On the third weekend of July, thousands of boats fill St. Mark's Basin to watch a spectacular fireworks show. The festival's origins date back to 1577, when the city celebrated its deliverance from the plague and the Palladian church was built on Giudecca Island in thanksgiving.

**Venice Film Festival.** Venice's Mostra del Cinema in late August or early September is one of the world's most important festivals dedicated to the seventh art. Actors, directors, and international celebri-

*Carnival in Venice is a marvelous time to become someone else.*

ties—pretty much everybody who's anyone in the world of the silver screen—arrive in the city to present new films and take part in a rich combination of cultural and social events. You might not be able to par-

ticipate in the festival premiere or hang out with your favorite stars, but most likely you'll see some of them as they populate the city and occupy the most prestigious hotels, like the Hotel Danieli.

## ON LOCATION VENICE

MOVIE: *Dangerous Beauty*
RELEASE: 1998
DIRECTOR: Marshall Herskovitz
CAST: Catherine McCormack, Rufus Sewell, Oliver Platt

I rate this as one of the most touching love stories of all time. For *Dangerous Beauty*, the city was dressed as the Venice of 1700, when kings and queens ruled Italy and secret love affairs between courtesans and the nobility could create scandals that even led to death. The movie tells the true story of Veronica Franco (played by Catherine McCormack), the daughter of a famous courtesan who wants to be different from her mother: Veronica wants to be a great wife and mother. She

falls in love with Marco (Rufus Sewell), from the ranks of high society, who had been promised in marriage to a rich woman he didn't love. Veronica and Marco establish a secret relationship, but in the end Marco breaks her heart by marrying another woman.

Veronica asks her mother to teach her all the secrets of being a courtesan, to prove to Marco that she could have any man in Venice—even the prince, or the king. Sweet little Veronica Franco becomes a courageous, sensual, and powerful woman, and Marco can't deny his heart any longer. He has to have her; but tragedy strikes, and the two face many obstacles to their being together. This is a powerful story that you can read about, even today, on one of the walls of the Grand Canal.

**Regata Storica.** On the first Sunday of September, one of the oldest and best loved events in Venice takes place on the Grand Canal. A spectacular procession of carved boats and costumed figures, led by the *bucentaur*, is followed by racing. For details, visit regatastoricavenezia.it.

**Venice Biennale**. The entire city gets involved in this world-famous event showcasing contemporary art. Exhibitions are staged over several months every other year (odd years) and include national pavilions from many countries. For details, visit labiennale.org/en.

## A Taste of the Past

While we were walking through the city , we came upon a unique restaurant right next to the Grand Canal, only a 15-minute walk from St Mark's Square. Called **Le Bistrot de Venise**, this phenomenal place offers a French-Venetian culinary experience that made a food aficionada like me feel like the queen of Venice! Le Bistrot de Venise serves elaborate meals reproduced from a French cookbook of the 14th century. You will feel like royalty after experiencing the marvelous service and course after course of exquisite food. From tender meats to delicate pastas and creamy desserts, I seriously have never eaten

*X marks the spot: The Church of San Barnaba, better known to movie fans as the library in* Indiana Jones and the Last Crusade.

### Tourist Hotel?

Angelina Joie and Johnny Depp check into Venice's Hotel Danieli in the 2010 movie *The Tourist*, but an elegant Venetian residence—Palazzo Pisani Moretta—was filmed as a stand-in for the hotel entrance. It would have been too difficult to shoot outside the real hotel, since it's only a few steps from busy St. Mark's Square. You do see the actual Hotel Danieli lobby in the movie, however.

## ON LOCATION VENICE

MOVIE: *Indiana Jones and the Last Crusade*
RELEASE: **1989**
DIRECTOR: **Stephen Spielberg**
CAST: **Harrison Ford, Sean Connery, Alison Doody, River Phoenix**

Indiana Jones fans will want to head to Campo San Barnaba, a little square in the Dorsuduro district across the Grand Canal from St. Mark's. You'll recognize the **Church of San Barnaba** facing the square as the library in *Indiana Jones and the Last Crusade*. The church dates from 1749, but the bell tower is quite a bit older. To the side of the square is the bridge that Indy walks toward, the Ponte dei Pugni. This is a pleasant, quiet square where you'll find places to eat and, in the Rio di San Barnaba, a floating vegetable market.

*Campo San Barnaba also features in the 1955 movie* Summertime, *when Katherine Hepburn falls into the canal here. Rossano Brazi was her costar in the movie.*

*Gondoliers compete in the Regata Storica.*

anything more delicious. It was a true Venetian feast, and the wines that accompanied each course were so good that even though I'm not a drinker, I couldn't help myself!

Celebrities were seated next to us, and the music of the gondoliers in the background were a beautiful reminder that I was in the country of love, where Italians pour amazing feeling into everything they do. When you go to this restaurant, ask for the owner, Giancarlo; he is an outstanding gentleman who will make your dinner the experience of a lifetime!

Of course, this is not an inexpensive place—it's a five-star restaurant, so be prepared to spend a lot of money. The wines are unique and expensive. But you know what, you only live...twice? It is worth every euro, dollar, or whatever money is your measure. Le

*The Regata Storica is a time when boats and boatmen wear their best.*

*Bistrot de Venise, a little bit of Paris in Venice.*

Bistrot de Venise is almost like dreaming while awake.

By the way, if you are getting married or planning your honeymoon, upstairs they have a party room that looks like an ancient museum, decorated in magnificent burgundy and red colors. Le Bistrot de Venise also rents out several high-end apartments in the heart of the city, equipped with all the comforts, elegant and luxurious.

**RESIDENZA BISTROT DE VENISE**
*San Marco,*
*Calle dei Fabbri 4690*
*30124 Venice*
**Website:** *residenza.*
   *bistrotdevenise.com*
**Phone:** *+39 041 5236651*

*The elegant and enchanting Londra Palace Hotel.*

*San Nicolo dei Mendicoli, featured in* Don't Look Now.

## ON LOCATION VENICE

MOVIE: *Don't Look Now*
RELEASE: **1973**
DIRECTOR: **Nicolas Roeg**
CAST: **Donald Sutherland,**
   **Julie Christie**

Easily my favorite of all Venice movies, *Don't Look Now* shows the darker side of the beautiful city. After the accidental death of their little girl, Laura (Julie Christie) and John Baxter (Donald Sutherland) decide to go to Venice, where he has agreed to take on the job of restoring a church. As the wife becomes friendly with a couple of nuns who tell her they can see the ghost of the little girl, the husband is stalked by a creepy-looking child. And in the background, a serial killer is prowling the Venetian streets. Everything plays out gradually, and nothing happens the way you expect it to. This is one of those amazing movies from the 70s that has sort of been lost in the sands of cinematic time, but it's worth seeking out.

Many atmospheric areas of Venice play a role in this haunting thriller. The church being restored by John Baxter is **San Nicolo dei Mendicoli**, a 12th-century brick structure on a tiny square—Campo San Nicolo—that's surrounded on three sides by canals. The Baxters' hotel in the film was a composite of two hotels on the Grand Canal: the Gabrielli Sandwirth for exterior and lobby scenes (Riva degli Schiavoni 4110) and the Bauer Grunwald for interior shooting (San Marco 1459). The funeral scene was filmed at the **church of San Stae**, facing the Grand Canal.

*Isn't this spectacular? This is the view from the rooftop of the Londra Palace.*

**Romina's Hotel Pick**

**Londra Palace Hotel.** To me, this is the number one place to stay in Venice, an extremely elegant hotel where each suite looks almost like a little museum. Not only have movies been shot right in front of the hotel, but stars often stay here. Among all the hotels I visited, this one remains in my heart. The staff speaks English and will make you feel right at home. A bonus: each of the sophisticated rooms has a book telling about movies that have been filmed in Venice.

While I was talking to Stefania, one of the hotel executives, I noticed a large glass wall behind us separating the lobby from the sumptuous dining room. Printed on the glass was my favorite thing in the entire world: music! I asked Stefania to tell me what music had to do with the hotel, and she said that one of the most famous composers in the world had once resided here: Peter Ilyich Tchaikovsky! Yes, the man who created *The Nutcracker*—one of my favorite composers, as I recall dancing to his amazing music as a little ballerina. In December 1877, the Russian composer stayed in room 106 and wrote the first three movements of his *Symphony No. 4.* You can stay in his suite! (As the story goes, Tchaikovsky would fight constantly with the hotel manager and lock himself in his room to stay inspired and write.)

The original core of the hotel building dates from 1853, when it was called the Hotel d'Angleterre & Pension. The roof was raised in the 1950s, and more recently the façade has been renovated. The draperies, the crystal chandeliers, the artwork, the ambiance—they give this charmed hotel a certain *je ne sais quoi*—something I can't really explain!

At the hotel's Do Leoni Restaurant, Chef Loris Indri combines the traditions of classic Venetian fare with more elaborate dishes. His culinary art is enhanced by the room's crystal and original paintings, and a spacious veranda looks onto the Riva degli Schiavoni. You want to live a Venetian life style? Then stay at this hotel. The food is to die for, and they have a sinful bar with unique concoctions and liqueurs!

**HOTEL LONDRA PALACE**
*Riva degli Schiavoni,*
*Castello 4171*
*30122 Venice*
**Website:** *londrapalace.com*
**Phone:** *+39 041 5200533*

## Getting to and around Venice

One of the more modern-looking structures in historic Venice is the Santa Lucia rail station, where more than 20,000 rail passengers pass through every day. The station is on the far northwest bank of the Grand Canal, and you can easily reach it by hopping on a vaporetto, the little water bus that for around $10 will take you to the station from Piazzale Roma (right after San Marco Square, recognizable because it's an area where cars park).

Venice is below sea level, so you won't see cars, but you will see many **gondolas**. These are romantic floating vessels to hop onto, but be prepared to pay around $100 dollars for a 30-minutes ride for two. Less expensive are the **vaporetti,** the boats considered to be Venice's city buses. They travel on regular routes, and the cost is around €7. If you're planning to visit several places in Venice, you might want to buy a vaporetto pass that lets you make multiple stops.

For crossing the canal where there's no bridge, there are **traghetti**, kind of a less-fancy version of gondolas. Other transportation options include **water taxis**, which are privately owned motorboats. For getting to or from the airport, a water taxi seating up to four people will cost around $130; for $100, you can hire one for a private tour of the entire city.

It can be challenging to get onto a water cab. I suggest that women wear pants and flat shoes, if possible. There are three little steps to make your boarding easier, but it can still be a bit tricky, so dress comfortably.

> **TRAVEL TIP** Twelve million tourists visit Venice each year, and many restaurants cook for the masses—focusing on quantity more than quality. If you really want the best, go to the restaurants I've talked about. Or stop for a bit of salami or cheese during the day, not ruining your appetite for a larger dinner but still enjoying traditional, locally prepared food.

> **TRAVEL TIP** For additional details about Venice, go to the city's official tourism site at veniceconnected.com. To find out about films, concerts, and other entertainment possibilities in the city, log on to aguestinvenice.com.

*Gondolas are the traditional, if pricey, way to see Venice. It may look touristy, but it's totally worth it.*

Have you ever wondered why the gondolas are all black? Because the law requires so! During the the 16th century, the canals of Venice were overcrowded with some 10,000 gondolas, and men of wealth and high class would try to outdo each other painting their boats with striking bold colors and designs. However, this started making Venice look a bit silly, so city officials passed a law decreeing that all gondolas must be painted black—no exceptions!

A fun and romantic thing to do is to take a late-afternoon or (even better) evening cruise on the Grand Canal—just like Angelina Jolie and Johnny Depp in *The Tourist*, or Veronica Franco and Marco in *Dangerous Beauty*. Tours usually last about two hours, and after dark the boats are all lit up (like in *The Phantom of the Opera*), creating a magical experience.

*The far less glamorous vaporetti are the practical and inexpensive city buses of Venice.*

 **Gondoliering 101**
One unique thing to do in Venice is to take a two-hour crash course on how to be a gondolier! Organized by an interesting tour company called Artviva, the classes are offered from March through November and cost about €80 per person. • Artviva, website artviva.com, phone +39 055 2645033.

*And just like a bus, you can catch a vaporetto along its regular route.*

*Traghetti will ferry you to the other side of the canal for a mere €2.*

## Did You Know?

No one is certain exactly how or when Venice's gondolas came into being, but they've been around at least since 1100. Once the principal form of transportation on the city's canals, the elegant-looking little boats now mostly carry sightseers.

Gondolas travel at a leisurely three miles an hour—about what we do when walking! They are all painted black, but each one has its own unique design and decorations. To me, the best time to ride a gondola is in the evening. The cost is pretty hefty, around €140 for a ride of 40 minutes, but the gondola can easily accommodate four to six people. If you want to serenade someone, though, you might want to leave two empty seats for a singer and a musician.

Here's something very funny about the gondoliers. If you're trying to arrange a good price, your gondolier will say that you must accept his price, or no ride. Then a friend of his will approach, pretending to be someone he doesn't know, and he'll offer you a better price! Settle on the fare before you board, then enjoy your ride.

# — *Cruising* THE COAST OF ITALY —

A world capital of trade in the Middle Ages and the Renaissance, Venice is a living reminder of the glories of Italy's long love affair with the sea. (It's no accident that America was discovered by an Italian! Although Columbus was from Genoa, Venice's arch-rival for commercial supremacy.)

One of the most magnificent ways to enter Venice is from the sea. While researching this book, I had the time of my life traveling through Italy aboard a marvelous small cruise ship, ending in Venice. Our arrival into the Venetian lagoon felt triumphant and quietly sumptuous, as if I was about to be elected queen of Italy! As you pass the main Mediterranean entry into the heart of the *serenissima*, a vision of pure beauty casts a powerful magic spell, and all the statues seem to change their cold and immobile look into one of wonder and marvel.

I had so much fun that I simply must share with you some of the highlights of the cruise, which departed from Barcelona, Spain, and stopped at many of the most beautiful spots on the Italian Riviera.

**Day One: Cinque Terre.** This rugged stretch of the Italian Riviera used to be the perfect place to hide from pirates. Cinque Terre means literally means "five lands," and the "lands" are five picturesque fishing villages. These are just wonderful villages, connected by trail, rail, and boat. Even if you come by boat there are many opportunities to hike, and you'll want to wear comfortable shoes. It's funny to witness some of the Italian women trying to hike in heels.

*Manorola, one of the five villages precariously perched above the sea in the Cinque Terre.*

Hey, it's all in the spirit of being a *bella donna*!

But if you're more like me and like what the Italians call *il dolce far niente*—the sweet feeling of doing nothing—you can go to the village of **Monterosso**, the only of the five that has a beach. The water in the Mediterranean is warm and so refreshing—not freezing like the Pacific Ocean where I live in Malibu, California! You can really enjoy swimming in the emerald green water and resting on the golden sand. I've been in this place many times, and all I want is for you to experience it, too. Keep in mind that because the government doesn't allow big hotels and resorts to be built

## ON LOCATION PORTOFINO

*The lovely—and expensive!—resort town of Portofino.*

MOVIE: *W./E.*
RELEASE: **2011**
DIRECTOR: **Madonna**
CAST: **Abbie Cornish, James D'Arcy, Andrea Riseborough**

I'll take a little break from the cruise to take you to the picturesque village of **Portofino** on the eastern side of the Italian Riviera. This enchanting place seems to have been created for people in love—but you'll need a loaded wallet to spend a few days here! Thinking about Portofino, I think about a movie that was shot here, a true story about an impossible love, a tragic love of sorts. I'm talking about King Edward VIII and his love affair with the sensual but fragile Wallis Simpson, the divorced American woman who convinced the King of England to abdicate his throne in order to marry her. The movie is *W./E.*, and Madonna directed it and won a Golden Globe for the song "Masterpiece" from the soundtrack.

Although this movie (brilliantly directed by Madonna, in my opinion) received truly horrible reviews, I found it charming, sensual, and even sad. The colors of the movie, the dialogue, and for sure the scenery in several parts of Europe and Italy make all the difference. I've received several letters from fans showing their appreciation for this movie. Because it truly touched me, I wanted to include it.

Portofino is where King Edward and Wallis Simpson, as shown in the movie (and as happened in real life), play on the beach and decide to let their love show. They hop on a beautiful yacht and set sail—just the most idyllic setting on earth, I believe!

"Portofino" comes from the ancient Latin name Portus Delphini, which means "Port of Dolphins." The best time to visit is June through September, as you'll want to swim in the bluest and warmest water you could ever find. You'll also want to see the **Christ of the Abyss** statue submerged in the water of a little bay just north of Portofino. Installed in 1954, the 8½-foot bronze statue was placed here to guard fishermen and SCUBA divers. Sculpted by Guido Galletti, it shows Jesus looking up toward the sky with open arms. Other local sights include the hilltop Church of St. George, housing relics of the village's patron saint.

*Monterosso is a picturesque place to relax on the beach.*

here, the small hotels in Cinque Terre vary in price and quality.

The cities of Levanto and Sestri Levante are grouped just north of Cinque Terre, and they are wonderfully relaxing and offer incredible panoramas. Out of Cinque Terre is the beautiful village of Santa Maria Ligure, from where a small boat can take you to the exclusive (and pricey) resort town of Portofino. This is where you are most likely to encounter famous and powerful people.

Traditional foods to enjoy in this area are pesto (that famous concoction of fresh basil, pine nuts, olive oil, and Parmesan cheese), stuffed ravioli, tortellini, and focaccias.

**Day Two**: **San Remo**. This was one of the few ports where we were able to actually dock, among rows and rows of extravagant yachts. Led by Italian guides well versed in their region's history, we took in San Remo's casino and the Cathedral of San Siro, finishing our walking tour in the oldest and quaintest part of the city, La Pigna. An afternoon bus tour took us to **Albenga** and its baptistery, ending at the Museo Civico Ingauno archaeological museum. This trip provided wonderful insight into how the people of San Remo live and work. This region's economy is based mostly on the production and export of extra-virgin olive oil. As our bus crisscrossed the steep hills and valleys, I couldn't help but marvel at how hard generations of people had worked to transform this challenging terrain into a productive agricultural area.

**Day Three: Vulci Archaeological Park.** We dropped anchor in Porto Santo Stefano for a day of touring the archaeological park. For those who enjoy exploring ancient tombs—some dating from the 8th century BC—this is the place to be! We started at Badia Castle, now housing a museum, and

*The town of Sestri Levante. On a good day, paradise might look a little like this.*

---

**TRAVEL TIP** One warning to those new to Italy: if you like to shop, do it early in the day, as Italians are devoted to their afternoon naps. Tourists or no tourists, many shops close for two hours or longer after lunchtime.

*A detail of the Etruscan frescos in the François Tomb.*

from there it was a short ride to an Etruscan site and then the extensive François Tomb. This tomb was discovered in 1857, its walls decorated with murals depicting early Etruscan events. After lunch at a shaded outdoor restaurant named Valle del Marta, we visited the quaint town of Tuscania to explore its picturesque weathered storefronts.

**Day Four: Agropoli and Paestum.** Heading southward, we were able to drop anchor in a port too small for the superliner set, giving us to access to what has to be one of the most impressive archaeological sites in all of Italy: Paestum. Founded in the 6th century BC, this Greek settlement is a World Heritage site, and rightly so. If ancient Greek architecture is

your cup of tea, Paestum is the whole pot! A half-hour drive delivered us to three amazingly preserved Greek temples—the temples of Hera (the oldest, around 550 BC), Neptune, and Athena. We also toured the adjacent museum.

**Day Five: Cefalu, Sicily.** The port and small town of Cefalu on Sicily's north coast is like a page out of a Robert Louis Stevenson novel. As our ship's tender made its way into this serene little harbor guarded by the ruins of a small fort built centuries ago, I could only wonder how many pirates and adventurers had made this same journey in times past! Director Giuseppe Tornatore shot one of the final scenes of *Cinema Paradiso* (see page

*The ruins of the temple complex in Paestum.*

*The church of San Pietro Caveoso dramatically rises from the rugged landscape of Matera.*

86) at this port. We took a 15-minute hike to visit Cefalu's majestic cathedral, begun in 1131 and finished about 30 years later. That something this impressive was built almost a thousand years ago staggers the imagination. May I say, "They just don't build them like they used to!"

Our buses next took us to Santo Stefano di Camastra, a small shopping boulevard known for its quaint pottery shops. Our final stop was at another of Sicily's fine baroque cathedrals, the "mother church" of Mistretta.

**Day Six: Matera.** When we reached the instep of

Italy's boot, our cruise offered two tour options: the ancient town of Matera and its cave dwellings, or the 7th-century Greek archaeological site of Metapontum. I chose Matera because more than 30 motion pictures have been filmed there, the most recent being Mel Gibson's 2004 film *The Passion of the Christ*. Gibson chose Matera because the pre-Christian cave-dwelling section of the city resembles what Bethlehem most likely looked like during Christ's lifetime.

We were able to enter three cave churches. The most fascinating part of the tour, however, was visiting one of the cave residences— complete with furniture and daily living utensils—where we saw how the people of Matera lived during the last century. The one we saw had been inhabited until the mid-1960s by a family with nine children, who lived there along with their donkey, goat, pig, and chickens. Such dwellings provided little more than shelter from the environment, but many were passed down from generation to generation until the early 1950s. At that time, due to the lack of proper sanitation, water, and other health issues, the government ordered the eviction of all the residents, giving them free housing in newer apartments in the city. The area sat dormant for a decade or two until it was designated as a UNESCO World Heritage site, when the government began to allow residents to reoccupy the caves

*A recreation of a traditional cave dwelling in Matera.*

*The trulli houses of Alberobello. The drawings on the beehive-shaped roofs aren't graffiti. Each one represents the name of a family living inside. For the people who live here, keeping the old traditions is very important.*

if amenities were brought up to modern-day standards. Several caves have been turned into cafés and small bed and breakfast inns—one of the most unique lodging experiences on the face of the earth, and maybe just your thing!

**Day Seven: Ostuni and Alberobello.** Heading up the heel of Italy's boot, the day began with a walking tour of Ostuni's Piazza della Liberta, the town hall, and the baroque Column of Saint Oronzo. One can never get enough of these quaint Italian villages! Another scenic ride took us to the **trulli houses** of Alberobello. Built centuries ago, many of these beehive-shaped buildings are

still family homes, while others have been converted into inns, restaurants, and shops. Excuse the pun, but for a trulli unique lodging experience, try booking a stay in one of these inns.

While we were enjoying the hot summer day, we stopped for a meal at a very good restaurant that I advise you to check out. It's called Ilo Trullo d'Oro, which means "the golden trullo." Inside, the fireplace is shaped just like the rooftops. • Ristorante Trullo d'Oro, Via F. Cavallotti 27, Alberobello, website trullodoro.it.

**Day Eight: Ortona.** An easy, one-hour bus ride took us through the **Abruzzo**, one of Italy's richest agricultural

areas. Green doesn't begin to describe its verdant patchwork of vineyards, olive orchards, and other crops. One gets the impression a divine hand helped create this Technicolor landscape of lovingly tended family farms, without a doubt the most lush farming area I have ever seen. Our first stop was at the cathedral at **Atri** to view its treasured 15th-century frescoes by Delitio in celebration of the life of the Virgin Mary. We happened to arrive just as a wedding party was entering the cathedral, allowing us to quietly witness a traditional Italian wedding— and causing me to ponder how many thousands of similar weddings have been performed here over the centuries.

At the Museum of Renaissance Instruments, we were treated to a performance of songs played on beautiful reproductions of several Renaissance string and accordion-type instruments. The tour highlight, however, was visiting the lower-level cellars to explore the ruins of the Roman foundations. Part of the original structure remains intact from the Roman period—when the cellar was used as a torture chamber, among other things. The completely restored area now serves as a unique contemporary art exhibition area. In this instance, the art was completely upstaged by the setting.

A quick bus trip deposited us at Don Ambrosio Restaurant for a five-course "traditional

*Performers in historic costume play the music of the Renaissance period at the Museum of Renaissance Instruments.*

Italian" lunch. The last excursion of the day was to **Chieti,** one of the region's most impressive cultural meccas. Set in a 19th-century villa is Chieti's Museum of Archaeology, containing some of the most amazing antiquities we saw on our entire cruise (dating back to the 6th century BC).

Contrary to what most people may think, Venetian blinds were invented by the Persians, not the Italians. But it was Venetian merchants who brought the blinds to Europe from Persia, hence the name Venetian blinds. The blinds became very popular during the 15th and 16th centuries. Venetians of that time loved to spy on people sailing down, and were now able to do so while keeping themselves from being noticed. Perhaps this love of anonymity helps explain Venetians' love for masks, especially during the famous Carnevale di Venezia.

# 11

# Florence, Tuscany, and the Heart of Italy

*"Not I, nor anyone else can travel that road for you. You must travel it for yourself."* — Walt Whitman

Traveling through Tuscany feels like a mystical encounter with paradise on earth. The landscape is mesmerizing: a succession of multicolor shades and forms, with vineyards and olive trees seeming to extend into infinity. If you want to find simplicity of life and inner peace, then this region in the heart of Italy is definitely the place to plant yourself! At the same time, the indulgent elegance of Florence and other ancient cities transforms the entire area into a living showcase of art and culture—the perfect place for anyone searching to experience something deep and meaningful.

*The magnificent dome on Florence Cathedral, designed in 1436 by Filippo Brunelleschi, is one of the great engineering triumphs of the Renaissance.*

## FLORENCE

The capital of Tuscany, Florence was the birthplace of the Renaissance in Italy. The most marvelous thing is that the city resembles an open-air museum. Why? Because you can find art practically everywhere, and you don't even have to buy a ticket! Everywhere you turn is

a surprise. You'll see incredible architecture at every corner. Florence is truly magnificent, and it is very hard to find the right words to describe it.

The skyline of Florence—or Firenze, as the Italians call it—is defined by the spectacular

**Brunelleschi Dome.** The immense brick and mortar dome over the cathedral of Santa Maria del Fiore—better known as the Duomo of Florence—is 142 feet across and soars 375 feet above the square. The cathedral itself was begun in 1296, but no one knew how to build a self-supporting dome big enough to cover it. In 1418 a contest was announced to find a solution. Filippo Brunelleschi—who'd studied the construction of Rome's Parthenon—was the winner for his design featuring a dome within a dome and an ingenious way of laying the bricks. The domed cathedral

**MOVIES**

Life Is Beautiful
Under the Tuscan Sun

was consecrated in 1436. • Piazza Duomo 17, website duomofirenze.it, phone +39 055 215380; admission to the cathedral is free, but there's a charge to visit the dome and climb the 463 steps to the top (reservations needed).

Across the piazza from the Duomo, you can admire the golden doors defined by Michelangelo as "the doors to paradise." The octagonal **Florence Baptistery**, built between 1059 and 1128, has three sets of bronze doors. Lorenzo Ghiberti's relief sculptures for the eastern set of doors are what inspired Michelangelo's description. The doors you see now are actually copies of the originals, which are in the **Museum of the Opera del Duomo** on the northeast side of the square.

Just to the south, the **Uffizi Museum** is one of the most amazing things to see in a city filled with stunning art. Its galleries trace a fantastic succession of history, with works by Botticelli, Giotto, Donatello, Michelangelo, Rembrandt, Rubens, Leonardo, and many others. Each day people from all over the world are crowded outside, doing whatever they can to get in! You *must* reserve your entrance time prior to arrival. You can ask your hotel to book it for you (they'll charge to do so), or you can book it yourself online. Some passes are good for a number of attractions. • Piazzale degli Uffizi 6 (between Palazzo Vecchio and the Arno River), website uffizi.org, phone +39 055 2388651;

*On the interior of the Brunelleschi dome is* The Last Judgment, *by Giorgio Varsari, commissioned in 1572 by Cosimo de' Medici.*

open Tuesday–Sunday from 8:15 am to 6:50 pm.

Nearby, the **Bargello Museum** displays sculptures by Michelangelo, Donatello, Giambologna, and others in the city's oldest government building (dating from 1255).

*The Florence Baptistery, built between 1059 and 1128, is one of the oldest buildings in Florence.*

*The Uffizi Gallery, home to some of the world's greatest works of art.*

• Via del Proconsolo 4; open 8:15 am to 1:50 pm (closed on the first, third, and fifth Sundays and the second and fourth Mondays).

Annunciation, *by Leonardo da Vinci, in the Uffizi.*

**TRAVEL TIP** There's a lot to see, so don't overwhelm yourself. Maybe a day of rest, out of many days spent walking around, will be good for you, with a nice meal and a glass of wine. Remember, Italy must be enjoyed like a beautiful bottle of wine, a little at a time. You should visit it several times to truly experience it all, and if that doesn't make you feel better, then think of me—born and raised in this beautiful country and *still* knowing very little about it! Don't despair if you can't see everything.

The Adoration of the Magi, *by Sandro Botticelli, one of the artistic masterpieces housed in the Uffizi.*

One of the treasures of the Bargello is this charmingly realistic bust of fifteenth-century politician Niccolò Uzzano, attributed to Renaissance sculptor Donatello.

Michelangelo was born only about 60 miles away, in the town of Caprese, in 1475. You'll see his influence and majestic work all over Florence. **Michelangelo's David** Is pure perfection. Housed in the **Academy Gallery** since 1873, the marble masterpiece originally stood in front of the **Palazzo Vecchio**, Florence's town hall. A replica took its place there when the statue was moved indoors. • Accademia di Belle Arti, Via Ricasoli 58–60; open Tuesday–Sunday, 8:15 am to 6:50 pm.

The Bargello Museum. Built in 1255, this building originally was the headquarters of the Podestà, the chief magistrate of the medieval city-state of Florence.

The famous Ponte Vecchio, with expensive shops on the bridge span.

If you're ready to take a break from museums, Florence has a lot to offer when it comes to shopping—everything high end and sophisticated. If you're someone who loves precious stones and amazing jewelry, you'll want to walk along the entire **Ponte Vecchio**, the oldest of the bridges over the Arno River (built in 1345). The stone span is famous for its jewelry shops selling the most expensive diamonds, gold pieces, watches, and other precious products.

In the area called **Santa Croce**, products in leather sell like hotcakes. Another popular area is **San Lorenzo**. By the way, if an Italian grabs you by the arm as he's trying to sell you something you can't find in his store, most likely he wants to take you around the corner to where he might have more choices. Don't worry, you aren't being kidnapped!

And of course, more food! **Mercato Centrale** is the place to go for great local produce and food products such as cheeses, pastas, and biscotti. The huge marketplace fills an iron and glass building that dates from 1874. It's off Via dell'Ariento a few blocks southwest of the Academy Gallery. • Monday–Saturday from 7 am to 2 pm, open later on Saturday.

## Getting to and around Florence

By road, Florence is about 175 miles from Rome, 185 miles from Milan, or 160 miles from Venice.

Florence has a small airport, Amerigo Vespucci, for European and domestic flights. The larger Galileo Galilei Airport in the city of Pisa is connected to Florence by frequent train service, a trip of about an hour. It's 52 miles west of Florence by road.

Florence is a major rail hub, and modern super-speed trains

*One of the world's greatest and most recognized works of art, Michelangelo's* David.

(called *frecciabianca*, *frecciarossa*, and *frecciargento*) cut travel time in half from Venice, Rome, or Naples. For schedules, visit <u>trenitalia.it</u>. You must have a reserved ticket for the high-speed trains, but you can usually book it at the station shortly before departure. You can also book tickets through Rail Europe at <u>raileurope.com</u> (there will be an extra charge to have them mailed to you).

Florence is equipped with great ground transportation, so it's easy to get wherever you want in the city on your own. The main attractions are within easy walking distance of the Santa Maria Novella train station.

*Entrance to the Mercato Centrale.*

## PISA AND ITS TOWER

Of course, when you go to Tuscany you'll want to visit Pisa to see its **Leaning Tower**. Begun in 1174 as the bell tower for the Cathedral of Pisa, the tower had already begun

### Italian Movie-Style Ice Cream

Italian gelato isn't as fattening as American ice cream, so you can eat it as much as you want...wrong! What I mean is that that Italian ice cream is made with natural ingredients and truly is not as supercaloric as the American version. It's a must—you need to enjoy it. As Julia Roberts says—eat, love, and then pray to lose the weight! Jokes aside, you're going to walk off everything you've been eating, so it's all good.

**Recipe**

  2 cups whole milk, divided (do not use low-fat or nonfat milk)

  2 tablespoons cornstarch

  1/3 cup granulated sugar

  Flavorings (extracts, pastes, fruit, chocolate, nuts, cookies—whatever you like)

1. Combine 1/4 cup of the milk with the cornstarch, whisking it until the cornstarch is dissolved and there are no lumps. Set aside.

2. Combine the remaining 1 3/4 cups milk with the sugar in a medium saucepan over medium heat, stirring constantly. Stir in the cornstarch mixture just as the sugar milk begins to boil. Reduce the heat and cook at a low simmer for 3 minutes, stirring constantly. Remove from the heat and allow to cool.

3. Pour the cooled mixture into a container, cover, and place in the refrigerator for at least 2 hours. Once it is cold, stir in your chosen flavorings and whisk until smooth.

4. Freeze the gelato mixture in an electric ice cream maker according to the manufacturer's instructions. You can also freeze it by pouring the chilled, whisked mixture into a shallow pan (such as a metal bread pan) or glass casserole dish. Place in the freezer for 30 minutes, then use a whisk or spatula to beat thoroughly, breaking up any ice chunks. Repeat every 30 minutes until your ice cream has a creamy consistency. This can take from 3 to 5 hours, depending on the freezer temperature and the pan depth.

tilting by the time the builders got to the third story, due to the sinking of the ground underneath. Political unrest combined with construction problems to delay completion until the mid-14th century.

In recent times the tower had been leaning a bit *too* much, so a major stabilization project was undertaken to keep it from bending over completely! Now you can once again climb the tower—all 294 steps—but you need to have a reservation to make sure you'll get in. You can make reservations at www. papisa.it.

Pisa has little tacky souvenirs, sorry to say, but how can you resist when you see those miniature Pisa towers? One for your mom, one for your aunt—oh, well.

## BAGNO VIGNONI

Don't look for a piazza in the middle of Bagno Vignoni village. Instead, there's a huge thermal pool, a 16th-century tank fed by waters bubbling up from an underground volcanic aquifer. You can't swim in this pool, but you can experience the same warm waters in the pools of Parco dei Mulini just steps away.

These hot springs were probably known back in Etruscan times, and we know the Romans used them—a plaque

*Bagno Vignoni was used as a location for the 1983 Russian-Italian film* Nostalghia, *directed by Andrei Tarkovsky.*

at the chapel of San Caterina testifies to the consecrating of the waters to the nymphs. In the 12th and 13th centuries, Bagno Vignoni was a stopping point for Christian pilgrims on their way to Rome. The thermal waters gained a reputation for curing various ailments, and the spa became a popular resort that drew such famed visi-

tors as Pope Pius II and Lorenzo the Magnificent.

The thermal village is about 65 miles south of Florence or 37 miles southwest of Cortona, just south of the town of San Quirico d'Orcia.

## Two Ancient Villages

If you are traveling from Florence to Rome, you must

*Beautiful, but built on sinking foundations: Pisa's world-famous Leaning Tower.*

*Arezzo's Piazza Grande, featured in* Life Is Beautiful.

stop at the little medieval town of **Ischia di Castro**! The ancient village (not to be confused with the island of Ischia, page 76) is surrounded by three deep valleys, and no road passes through its historical center, adding to a deep sense of peace permeating one's soul. Minutes

 **TRAVEL TIP** The best time to visit Tuscany, and in particular Cortona, is in May. Winters are too cold, and sometimes snow makes it impossible to drive around then or enjoy the beauty of this region on foot.

## Life is Beautiful in Tuscany

The Tuscan people are the most loving and fun people! Roberto Benigni, leading actor and director for the 1997 movie *Life Is Beautiful*, is from Tuscany. If you know how entertaining he is, then you have an idea how wonderful Tuscans are—just amazing people, who love to share their rich culture with the world.

*Life Is Beautiful* was shot entirely in Tuscany and Umbria. The city of **Arezzo** (about 40 miles southeast of Florence) plays a major role, as the place where Guido (played by Benigni) wants to open his bookstore. Signs now identify various locations used in the movie, including the main square, Piazza Grande. About 15 miles south in the town of **Cortona,** the Teatro Signorelli opera house is where Dora (Nicoletta Braschi, Benigni's real-life wife) first captures Guido's attention.

This movie won Oscars for Benigni as best actor, for best foreign film, and for best score.

*Roberto Benigni, director and star of* Life Is Beautiful.

away, other quaint villages nestle among the Tuscan hills. Life here has a rhythm that flows with the seasons: harvesting grapes in fall, hunting wild boar in winter (for making fresh sausage), making wine in spring, harvesting vegetables and fruits all summer. This place is full of history and beauty—you're going to love it!

Ischia di Castro is about 88 miles south of Florence and 58 miles northwest of Rome.

Another ancient village lies 38 miles to the east. Founded by the Etruscans more than 2,500 years ago, **Civita di Bagnoregio** is called "the dying city" because it sits high atop an eroding volcanic mountain that looks as if it might fall into pieces at any second. Only 20 people still live in the rustic village year-round, though in summer that jumps to 300 because of city-dwellers who spend vacations here. You can walk up the steep hill to the village over a footbridge (cars aren't allowed) from the newer, larger sister town of Bagnoregio. It is a strange but beautiful place to see.

### Did You Know?

Olives hand-picked in the hills around Frances Mayes' Villa Bramasole are made into the most delicious and nutritious olive oil you will ever taste! In case you're not near Bramasole, you can order the olive oil from thetuscansun.com.

## ON LOCATION TUSCANY

MOVIE: *Under the Tuscan Sun*
RELEASE: 2003
DIRECTOR: Audrey Wells
CAST: Diane Lane, Sandra Oh, Raoul Bova

What woman didn't fall in love with Marcello and feel part of the life of broken-hearted Frances, played by Diane Lane? Sometimes we need to run away from all that is surrounding us, from the pain and the tears, and have the brave attitude to start all over again, to follow our fantasy and believe that all things are possible. This is the movie *Under the Tuscan Sun*.

*In the market scene filmed for* Under the Tuscan Sun, *prices are shown in lire, though the euro was introduced in 2002.*

A number of locations in Tuscany were shown in the movie, but the centerpiece was the lovely hill town of **Cortona**, about 72 miles southeast of Florence. Remember the Italian villa that Frances fell in love with during a bus trip in the province of Arezzo? Well, it does exist, though the real Villa Bramasole—the one Frances Mayes wrote about in her book *Under the Tuscan Sun*, on which the movie was based—wasn't used for filming. You can see both the actual Bramasole and its movie stand-in, which is called Villa Laura and has been remodeled since the movie was made (in fact, you can rent it). The lovingly restored villa that became Frances Mayes' home is outside of town, uphill off Viale Passerini; ask for directions at the tourist information office in town, and they'll provide a map. And if you like to walk, another outing will take you to a beautiful stone monastery and chapel founded in the early 13th century by Saint Francis, called **Le Celle**. It's about a 45-minute walk from town.

Two other Cortona sites you'll recognize from *Under the Tuscan Sun* are the Teatro Signorelli opera house and the Piazza della Republica, the square where the outdoor market and the Christmas scene took place. The striking 9th-century Farneta Abbey, outside of town on the road to Foiano, is also shown in the movie. Other Tuscany locations in the film include Florence, Siena, and Montepulciano.

*The medieval hill town of Montepulciano about 20 miles southwest of Cortona, where Frances watched flag-throwers in* Under the Tuscan Sun, *was also the setting for the 2009 Twilight Saga movie* New Moon.

Cellars below the houses in the village extend deep into the volcanic tufo rock, forming caves where the temperature is ideal for keeping wine and preserving foods. The locals take pride in offering visitors samples of their products—and some of the best olive oil in Italy comes from this region.

---

*Civita and Bagnoregio were filming locations for the 2008 movie* Pinocchio, *directed by Alberto Sironi and starring Bob Hoskins as Geppetto. Federico Fellini shot important scenes here for his classic 1956 film* La Strada.

---

*The thermal pool in Bagni Vignone.*

*This footbridge is the only access to the village of Bagnoregio.*

## Romina's Hotel Pick

At **BB Fiore**, you can enjoy a charming bed and breakfast arrangement in Ischia di Castro. The owner is a wonderful American woman who will make sure that you feel comfortable and welcomed. BB Fiore is right in the historical center of the village, providing a lovely escape from the typical tourist scene. Less than 20 miles away are the Saturnia hot springs, known for their healing properties; custom health packages can be designed for guests. There are also endless walking and hiking trails in the surrounding hills and valleys, or you can see the area on a bicycle. Guides are available for cycling, walking, and visiting nearby villages.

**BB FIORE**
*Via del Fiore*
*Ischia di Castro 01010*
**Website:**
   *www.bbfiore-idro.com/en*
**Phone:** *+39 345-0743478;*
   *(818) 991-4453 from the U.S.*

# Photo Index

# Index

# Romina Arena

From being a Mouseketeer for Disney's "Topolino" in Italy to becoming celebrated as "the Queen of Popera," **Romina Arena's** multiple talents have inspired millions across the world. Romina has sold over four million records worldwide and has received many major honors, including a Global Citizenship Award from the United Nations in recognition of her humanitarian support for the children of Haiti. And her ability to write, speak, and sing fluently in ten different languages has allowed her to become not only a successful music artist, but an international authority in the travel industry, as well.

In 2012, Romina reunited with her longtime mentor, legendary Oscar, Grammy, and Golden Globe award winning film composer Maestro **Ennio Morricone**, who allowed her to write and sing lyrics to his some of his famous movie scores. The duo collaborated together on *Morricone.Uncovered*, which was released September 2012 on Perseverance Records. When asked why he decided to work with Romina on this project, Morricone was quoted in the *Malibu Times* as saying, "I decided to work with Romina because of her hard work and incredible successes. But most importantly, I consider her the most dominant voice I have heard in my life. I do not allow just any artist to write lyrics to my movie scores. But for her I make the exception."

*Where Did They Film That? Italy* is Romina Arena's first book. And the book's companion album, *Where Did They Film That? Italy—The Music Journey* was released in April 2016 by Lakeshore/Sony Records. For more information on Romina Arena, visit **www.RominaArena.com**.